LEARN,
DON'T STUDY

'Learning makes us better human beings and helps the evolution of civilizations. It's not just about information and data. Our civilization has flourished because we are continually evolving and learning. In Pramath's book you will find a wonderful collection of inspired wisdom, reality and hope. I hold his profound and courageous book to my heart, reminded of life's non-stop teachings'—**Kailash Satyarthi**, founder, Bachpan Bachao Andolan; and Nobel Peace laureate (bachelor's in electrical engineering)

'Pramath Raj Sinha draws on his immense experience in the corporate world and, more tellingly, from the world of education to write this extremely important book. He emphasizes the importance of learning, which is a journey without an end. I also think that this book is unique, because no other book that I know of has addressed the questions and issues that this book discusses. The style is simple and jargon-free. I am sure readers will find it useful and will learn by debating with the author's views'—**Rudrangshu Mukherjee**, chancellor and professor of history, Ashoka University (bachelor's in history)

'The twists and turns of my career could very well be a case study for this book. From having an opportunity to study engineering to switching to economics, account servicing in my first job, studying management, becoming a journalist and teacher, and all the while turning entrepreneur and, eventually, Internet investor, at no stage could I ever have predicted where I would end up. Yet it all adds up. Drawing on his vast experience in guiding young minds, Pramath provides rich insights for students and their parents as they make critical choices about education and careers, particularly in today's context. If you are deciding what to study or where to work next, this is the book for you'—**Sanjeev Bikhchandani**, founder and executive vice chairman, Info Edge (naukri.com); founder and trustee, Ashoka University; and Padma Shri awardee (bachelor's in economics)

'Pramath has captured the essence of how students need to think about higher education and careers today. In fact, *Learn, Don't Study* advocates several of the ideas that I have consistently espoused in my long years as an educator. As his high-school teacher, I pushed Pramath to go beyond his comfort zone and build his leadership skills outside the classroom. Starting from a young age, this has worked wonders for countless students I have had the privilege to teach and mentor. This book should be essential reading for all high-school students, especially those who are looking for guidance and direction'—**Gowri Ishwaran**, adviser, Shiv Nadar Foundation; vice-chair, The Global Education and Leadership Foundation; founder–principal, Sanskriti School, New Delhi; and Padma Shri awardee (bachelor's in English literature)

'Having a squiggly career, as a non-techie, non-MBA founder–CEO of an online company, has surprised me and those who know me. Yet, it has been an incredible journey: at once, bizarre and incredibly natural, and its wonders, magic and potential can be for everyone, with some courage, conviction and serendipity. Live such careers and enable them. Pramath's book is a great primer, rich in anecdotes and wisdom, as only he can weave and craft, with his masterful storytelling and unique generosity of words and spirit'—**Shreyasi Singh**, founder and CEO, Harappa Education (bachelor's in history)

'The best gift Indian students and parents could get from Pramath. From his decades of having collected very unique dots, he has connected them in this beautifully written book. *Learn, Don't Study* will build belief, courage and confidence in our students to chart learning and life journeys they're most likely to succeed with. Pramath has stitched together wisdom from his decades of experience with students and their careers. This book will serve as a guide for parents and students in making some of the most important decisions of their lives'—**Atul Satija**, founder and CEO, The/Nudge Foundation; and CEO, GiveIndia Organization (Indian School of Business, class of 2004, and bachelor's in mechanical engineering)

'This book humanizes the discovery process and comforts you. It's a must-read because it is real, reflective and relatable. I spent the first quarter of my life confused about myself and my passion. I wanted to be an architect but studied economics and worked with a bank. But today I am nurturing my passion, which I have developed over the past decade—helping transform Indian higher education. In between are the chapters and stories in this book that speak to me. This path of picking up and connecting the dots while being a beneficiary of Pramath's mentorship has been a fulfilling one. I wholeheartedly support the argument that anyone can achieve anything'—**Karan Bhola**, director, Young India Fellowship (YIF), Ashoka University (YIF, class of 2013, and bachelor's in economics)

'*Learn, Don't Study* is a practical guide for anxious students and their equally anxious parents in the New World. As a '90s kid, when I insisted on pivoting from engineering to data analytics to brand strategy in my mid-twenties, I was met with appalled looks, and even more so when I quit my high-paying brand consulting job to join a D2C textile start-up during the pandemic. It only made me more unsure and stressed about my career choices. With real-world examples, Pramath beautifully explains how this need to pivot is normal and healthy even. He gives you a way to constructively look at your career conundrum. Pramath always says, "Be comfortable with uncertainty," and it's a life advice I'll carry forever. This book will tell you why that's important and just how exactly to do that'—**Ashmita Kannan**, chief brand officer, A Toddler Thing (Vedica Scholars Programme for Women, class of 2016, and bachelor's in computer science)

'As Albert Camus said, "You cannot acquire experience by making experiments. You cannot create experience. You must undergo it." This book is indispensable in understanding how to make a life worth living. Dr Sinha has vividly put forth the importance of sowing the seed of the superpower, curiosity and the need to develop "soft skills", which ultimately drive lifelong learning in today's times. I highly recommend this book to all students and parents who are confused about the right path after school. This will be a guide on that blurry path'—**Mingur Angmo**, principal, Druk Padma Karpo School, Shey, Ladakh (Naropa Fellowship, class of 2016, and bachelor's in history)

'I was lucky to be mentored by Pramath while I was making a huge career pivot—a privilege enjoyed by a select number of young seekers. But this book reaches out to millions across the world eager to make sense of themselves and the multiple ways in which they could work and actualize themselves. You're going to love this book because it brings together the expertise of Pramath, a pool of incredible interviews and a true Indian perspective. The book is an eye-opener not just for students trying to build squiggly careers but also for parents still caught up in a world of dated paradigms'—**Rutvi Ashar**, associate director, Communications and Operations, Institute of Regenerative Medicine, Penn Medicine (Anant Fellowship, class of 2018, Anant National University, and bachelor's in architecture)

LEARN,
DON'T STUDY

*A Guide for Students & Parents to Succeed
in the Ever-Changing Landscape
of the Modern Workplace*

PRAMATH RAJ SINHA

BUSINESS

An imprint of Penguin Random House

PENGUIN BUSINESS

USA | Canada | UK | Ireland | Australia
New Zealand | India | South Africa | China

Penguin Business is part of the Penguin Random House group of companies
whose addresses can be found at global.penguinrandomhouse.com

Published by Penguin Random House India Pvt. Ltd
4th Floor, Capital Tower 1, MG Road,
Gurugram 122 002, Haryana, India

First published in Penguin Business by Penguin Random House India 2023

ISBN 9780670097487

Typeset in Sabon by Manipal Technologies Limited, Manipal
Printed at Thomson Press India Ltd, New Delhi

www.penguin.co.in

In loving memory of Amma and Babuji,
Sheela and Udaya Raj Sinha.
Their values and actions shaped who I became.
Now that they are gone, I am reminded of
their impact on my career every day.

'The way we talk to our children becomes their inner voice.'

—Peggy O'Mara

'The way we talk about them becomes their life stories.'

—Shelja Sen

Contents

Introduction

Making the 'Right' Choice

'What should I study to best prepare myself for success in today's working world?'

This is the most common question I get from young people (and the parents of those) who are transitioning from their school to college. They want to know what fields they should study, what universities or programmes to attend and what career track would give them the best chance to succeed. They want to ensure that they make the 'right' choice for their future, or, in most cases, avoid the 'wrong' one.

But while most people are looking for a simple, black and white response, my answers are far from straightforward.

Why?

This is because the professional world isn't as straightforward as it once was, especially in India. The modern workplace is changing rapidly. While many of my generation chose a career in engineering or medicine or business and then stuck to it, most people entering college today will end up changing their careers multiple times. In fact, according to the Michael Page India Employment Intentions report, Indians change jobs more frequently than any other country with 47 per cent of those surveyed in 2016 saying they had changed jobs within the last six months.[1] The average worker today will have several jobs over the course of their lives and that number is on the rise. Many of the careers that young people will have in the future don't even exist yet.

These 'squiggly' careers, as American authors Sarah Ellis and Helen Tupper call them, are becoming the new norm. And this new work paradigm has created considerable confusion for young people and their parents, as they attempt to prepare for and chart their future.

The Pressure to Succeed (and Conform)

One of the biggest challenges that young people face today is that while the world around them is changing, the pressure on them to succeed is as high as ever. According to a UNICEF-Gallup international survey for the Changing Childhood Project, 58 per cent of India's young people believe that children today experience more pressure to succeed than their elders did.[2] In this high-pressure environment, it is difficult for students to put in the requisite work, experimentation and self-reflection to figure out which career path is best suited for them. As a result, many continue to walk down the well-trodden paths of engineering, medicine or business, with little attention given to how they might best prepare themselves for the true realities of the modern workplace.

This pressure is emanating from many sources, but from parents more than any other. Many from my generation remember what it was like before India's economy exploded onto the world stage in the late 1990s and early 2000s, and thus they want their children to have the success they've achieved in their own lives. The parents who come to me for answers are often desperate to ensure their children succeed; and the way that they define that success tends to be quite narrow: focusing more on financial stability rather than personal fulfillment and coming through limited professional paths. Unfortunately, this narrow perspective has trickled down to our children. A 2019 survey by the online career counselling platform Mindler, for example, found that 93 per cent of the 10,000 students surveyed were unable to think of more than seven career paths.[3]

This continued social pressure has created an unfortunate paradox. Never have there been more opportunities for young people to find meaningful and successful careers outside the traditional pathways. And yet, especially here in India, very few of our young people are thinking broadly, or creatively, about their future and there aren't enough structures in place to prepare students for the dynamic and ever-changing careers of the future.

Institutions Are Struggling to Keep Up

Making educational choices in this brave new world can often feel like trying to hit a moving target. Many of the old assumptions about education and careers are becoming outdated and our educational institutions are struggling to provide young people with the support and guidance they need to thrive in this rapidly changing environment.

According to the Hechinger report, large tech employers like Microsoft and Linux are getting impatient with universities because they are not preparing students for the jobs they need filled. Instead, they're taking matters into their own hands by partnering with companies like edX and creating courses themselves.[4] One of the primary reasons for starting my own company, Harappa Education, was to help address this educational gap in India, where the shift to online learning is impacting traditional universities.

While I'm a firm believer in the value of traditional education, I am well aware that these institutions need to evolve to keep up with the changing marketplace. At the same time, students need to be more actively engaged in their educational endeavours. Gone are the days when they could simply pick a major and follow it towards a successful career. Agility and adaptability are key to success in the modern educational and career worlds.

Today's students and their parents need new guides and a set framework to make decisions about what educational opportunities to pursue and what to focus on as they embark on their professional journeys.

That's what inspired me to write this book. Drawing on my experiences working in the field of education for nearly twenty-five years as the founder of ISB, Ashoka University, Harappa and several other programmes, this book pulls together the best and most practical advice available for young people (and their parents) who are facing some of the most important—and challenging— choices of their professional lives.

Practical Advice from Those Who've Succeeded

While the book is based on my own experience, in both the professional and educational worlds, it's much more than that. I don't want you to simply take my advice at face value, so I interviewed an inspiring group of individuals who have navigated (and are navigating) the modern career landscape, asking for their perspective on what has helped them to succeed and what advice they have for young aspirants who are just starting out.

In doing so, I hope to provide you with a wide variety of examples of what a successful career can look like. Some of the interviewees started down traditional paths. Others were innovators from the very beginning. Some are younger professionals, in the middle of their own journeys. Others are nearing the end of their working lives. Many of the interviewees were educated in India, while others attended schools abroad. While you may never have heard of most of the interviewees, they are all extraordinary people in their own way. And all of them share one thing in common: they have never stopped growing and evolving, personally or professionally.

I wanted to focus my interviews on people with a direct connection to India, whether through birth, family or education, in order to highlight the unique cultural experience that we have in this country. Whereas so much of what has been written about career development comes from the West, I wanted to present an approach that was uniquely Indian.

The talented array of people I interviewed include:

- **Monica Hariharan:** A journalism graduate, whose dedication to doing something fun and meaningful with her life eventually led her to help grow a UK-based food delivery start-up.
- **Siya Sood:** A bright young professional in the education sector whose mentors helped her to uncover her hidden talents and launched her into the next phase of her career.
- **Smridhi Marwah:** A PhD student with a passion for lifelong learning that led her from a biomedical sciences degree to a successful career in the non-profit sector.
- **Nikhil Sud:** An Indian native whose passion for critical thinking led him to the US to pursue a liberal arts education, a law degree, legal practice and a position at a top strategic advisory firm in Washington DC.
- **Ambika Nigam:** An economics graduate, whose early work experience inspired her to start her own online career path discovery company to help others discover what they're best at and turn it into a successful and fulfilling career.
- **Anita Mackenzie:** An interior designer whose late-in-life career pivot combined her corporate background with her lifelong passions.
- **Paroma Roy Chowdhury:** A 'shapeshifter' whose penchant for taking on new challenges has led her from business journalism to corporate communications to the fast-changing world of EdTech.

- **Uday Shankar:** A well-known media giant whose career started in journalism and culminated in running one of India's largest entertainment companies, and now founding a multi-billion-dollar investment platform.
- **Srikant Sastri:** A serial entrepreneur whose passion for mentorship has driven him to help countless young people get started on their own career journeys.

My approach to these interviews was to remain very open and curious, leaving my own ideas at the door so I could find out what made each interviewee tick. I asked them a variety of questions about how they prepared themselves for their careers, what were the key lessons they learned along the way and what advice they have for young people who are just starting out.

Their answers were deeply insightful and over time, I started to notice patterns in what they had to say. Each of the people I spoke to cited similar qualities, principles and experiences that had helped them to achieve success in their own squiggly careers. As a result of these conversations and the lessons that I've learned in my own career, I distilled a series of core insights that I believe are most useful for young people who are making important decisions about their education and professional pathway.

These insights make up the framework for the book. In each chapter, we explore one key principle both through my own experiences and those of the interviewees. We talk about why it's important and more importantly, how to apply it to your own life and career. Along the way, there are plenty of practical tips and tools to put these insights into practice in your own life.

As you make your way through the book, I encourage you to remain as open as possible. One of the most cited qualities mentioned by all the interviewees is agility, or the ability to adapt and change throughout one's career. Agility starts with openness. Try to see yourself and your career, as a blank canvas upon which you can paint a beautiful picture. The more you can do this, the further you will be able to go.

I hope you enjoy the journey!

1

You Can Do Anything

Introduction

In the final season of the hit American TV show *This Is Us*, there's a powerful scene that I think most young people today can relate to. The scene takes place in one of the show's many famous flashbacks–this time to the early 2000s, when the three main characters, triplets Kate, Kevin and Randall Pearson, are all twenty-ish and just beginning their adult lives. 'The Big 3', as their late father Jack lovingly dubbed them, spend the evening in the abandoned swimming pool where they had spent their summers during childhood, each reflecting on their respective life trajectories.

While the two brothers have their own struggles, they have each already chosen a career trajectory: Kevin has moved to Los Angeles to pursue acting and Randall is attending Carnegie Mellon University so he can eventually 'change the world'. Kate, on the other hand, is still wayward, living at home with their grieving mother and waiting tables at a local diner.

In a particularly vulnerable moment, Kate opens up to her two brothers and admits that she has no idea what she wants to do with her life. She reveals that seeing the two of them being so clear about their life's passions is making her feel like something is wrong with her.

'When I look into my future,' she says, 'I literally see nothing.'

Most of Us Don't Know and That's Okay

The truth is that in the real world, most of us are far more like Kate than her two brothers, especially during our transition from adolescence to adulthood when we first leave the nest and start to test out our wings. During this stage of life, most of us don't understand ourselves, or the world, well enough to have a clear vision of our future. We might have an inkling about what we like and dislike or about the things we're good at and not so good at, but we just don't have enough experience to translate those feelings into a clear vocational path.

Unfortunately, many of us draw the same conclusion that Kate did and assume that there must be something wrong with us if we don't know exactly what we want to do with our lives. I've spoken with countless young people in a similar predicament who feel as if they need to figure it all out in advance. They're afraid that if they don't, they'll get left behind by all the people around them that seem to have it all figured out. The sad reality is that this mindset is often reinforced by their support systems—parents, educators and peers—who all seem hellbent on pressuring the young people in their lives into choosing a career long before they're even ready.

The good news is that it's possible to solve this dilemma and discover what you want to do with your life, even if you're like Kate and don't know what you want to do yet. That's what this book is all about. All of the professionals I've interviewed have found their own unique solution to this career conundrum and have discovered vocations that have brought them success, fulfillment and purpose. Some knew what they wanted to do from a young age itself. Others discovered it along the way. Still others ended up wanting to do many different things and pursued multiple careers.

Don't Be Overly Concerned with Money

Before we go any further in this chapter, I want to address one of the primary obstacles to building a passion-based career. That is, obsessing about how much money you will make.

Don't get me wrong, I'm not suggesting that financial compensation isn't an important aspect of your career. It is one of the key by-products of being successful. In fact, a now-famous 2010 study by Angus Deaton and Daniel Kahneman (author of the bestselling book *Thinking, Fast and Slow*) found that the old adage that 'money can't buy happiness' isn't always true. They found that up to a certain level of income, the more money you make, the happier you will be. But once you cross a certain income threshold, which at the time of the US-based study was $75,000 annually, most of your basic needs are met and making more money is less predictive of happiness than doing something you enjoy.[1] So while earning a comfortable living should be a factor as you ponder your professional future, it shouldn't be the primary criterion, especially when you're starting out.

In my experience, I have found that many young people tend to become myopic about how much money they could make within certain career paths. As a result, they make poor choices about what to study, which schools to attend or what jobs to take up. If money is your top criterion for determining what you want to do with your life, what educational path to take or what job offer to choose, it can often stand in the way of a deeper, more fulfilling and ultimately more successful career.

This phenomenon is particularly strong in India. As one of my interviewees, Siya Sood, suggests, there is a tremendous fear of poverty in this country. We live in a deeply mixed society where everywhere you go, from the poshest neighbourhoods to the poorest slums, there are reminders of extreme poverty. She recounted the story of how, when she was young, her parents would point at beggars on the street and warn her that if she didn't make enough effort in school, she would end up like them. This culturally conditioned fear can often lead young people to become overly anxious about their financial stability, often at the expense of their long-term happiness.

In the early stages of your career, the most important thing you can do is to gain experience, and in doing so, start to discover your passions and strengths. You should learn and develop skill sets that will benefit you throughout your career. By building this strong foundation, you would set yourself up for more success in the long run; and part of that success will be financial. Money should be a symptom of a well-rounded and successful career.

Anything Is Possible, with a Twist

One of the most important piece of advice I have to offer young people is that it's possible to do anything with your life. If you work hard, learn from your experiences and remain open to possibilities, you can build a successful career doing something you are deeply passionate about.

But over the years I've learned that simply saying 'you can do anything' isn't enough, especially for the Kates of the world, who don't know what 'anything' actually means for them. In fact, being told 'you can do anything' can, for many of us, make things worse. So, I've refined my advice and developed three core principles:

1. It's possible to make a career out of doing something you love.
2. Your passion is usually something you develop.
3. You can have multiple loves and multiple careers.

Together, these core principles are meant to help you think about yourself and your career in a more dynamic context. Rather than forcing you to discover your vocation in advance, they are meant to liberate you from that 'fixed' mindset and open you up to a new way of viewing your career–one that is more like an explorer seeking to discover your passions and aptitudes as you move forward on your journey.

Let's explore these three principles in depth.

You Can Do Something You Love

Most of us are likely familiar with some version of the saying, 'do what you love' or its cousin phrase, 'follow your passion.' Variations of these platitudes adorn everything from t-shirts and coffee mugs to the mottos of uber-progressive companies. We often hear successful people like professional athletes or musicians say they are grateful for being paid to do something they love. Others talk about how when they go to work it doesn't 'feel' like work because they are so passionate about their vocation.

This mindset towards work is popular for a reason. For many of us who are fortunate enough to get good education, the world is filled with more opportunities than ever before. We don't have to simply settle for a stable career that pays the bills, regardless of whether we like it or not. According to a 2020 report by Wunderman Thompson about the attitudes of Generation Z, 70 per cent are more interested in doing something meaningful with their lives than they are, in making money.[2] Indeed, it's becoming more and more common for the 'average' person who doesn't have some exceptional talent like an athlete or artist to create deep and meaningful careers that they are passionate about. The definition of a passion-based career has significantly expanded and evolved to include a wide variety of options.

This trend towards pursuing passion-based careers has accelerated during the COVID-19 pandemic. One of the key factors behind what people are calling 'the great resignation' is that the pandemic gave many people the opportunity to step back and reflect on their lives, often leading them to leave their existing jobs for new and more fulfilling lines of work. In an August 2021 feature for the *New Indian Express*, Smith Verma interviewed a wide range of people who used the pandemic as an opportunity to pursue their passions, including a Mumbai-based engineer who quit her job at a start-up to launch her own cat-themed clothing and accessory company, a VP at a multinational insurance firm who left his career of thirty years to start his own law firm and a real estate veteran who pivoted into a career as an online food and beverage influencer.[3]

Similarly, everyone I interviewed for this book has built at least one career out of doing something they love. And that looks different for each of them. There's Monica, whose steadfast dedication to doing something both meaningful and fun eventually led her to help found an online food delivery company. Srikant, who discovered his passion for entrepreneurship and leveraged that into a successful career in which he started and sold multiple companies and now serves as a mentor to other aspiring entrepreneurs. Or Uday, whose passion for social change led him to journalism and eventually into a star-studded career in media. Then there's Ambika, who started an online career path discovery company to help people build their own passion-based careers.

One of the primary reasons I chose to interview these individuals for the book is because they had all found, in their own ways, careers that they were passionate about. I wanted to highlight this aspect of each of their careers to show you that it truly is possible to 'do what you love', if you're dedicated to it. They are living proof that you don't have to simply accept a job or profession for the sake of stability or financial compensation alone. You truly can discover your passion and turn it into a vocation.

But as we'll explore in the next principle, most of us don't take the right approach to discovering our passion or doing what we love.

SIDEBAR: The Young India Fellowship

In 2011, I helped to launch the Young India Fellowship (YIF) at Ashoka University to help meet the growing demand for socially conscious leaders by training students in a multidisciplinary, real-world approach to social change. YIF is a year-long residential programme that offers students a postgraduate diploma in liberal studies that is based in experiential learning through various projects in a variety of different sectors. Our faculty is world-class and brings their diverse experiences from prestigious universities around the globe.

Thus far, we have been thrilled with the results. Over the past decade YIF has helped graduate 2,000 fellows and assisted many to find placements at a wide variety of institutions, including the World Bank, McKinsey and Company, Deloitte, the World Wildlife Fund and Amnesty International. In addition to placements, our fellows have been awarded many prestigious grants, including the Rhodes, Gates, Fulbright and Commonwealth Scholarships. Social entrepreneurship is a big part of the

YIF curriculum and many of our graduates have started ventures of their own, including a start-up that develops low-cost tablets for use in Indian schools.

Your Passion Is Usually Something You Develop

While 'do what you love' and 'follow your passion' are important principles to keep in mind as you build your own career, they don't actually end up being very good advice. And there's some very interesting research to back this up.

In a 2018 article for the *Psychological Science Journal*, authors Paul O'Keefe, Carol Dweck and Gregory Walton suggest that there are two general approaches to building a passion-based career; finding your passion or developing it. And their research found that the latter tends to be much more effective than the former. They suggest the idea that each of us has a unique passion that we are meant to discover represents more of a 'fixed mindset'. On the other hand, viewing your passion, or passions, as something you develop and cultivate, represents more of a 'growth mindset'.

They conducted a series of studies and found some key reasons why it is better to have this growth mindset than a fixed one. First off, if you think you have only one unique passion, you're much less likely to pursue other opportunities when they present themselves to you, which can limit your potential in the long run. And second, those with fixed beliefs about their passion have more difficulty continuing to grow when their passion inevitably wanes throughout their career. 'Urging people to find their passion may lead them to putting all their eggs in one basket only to then drop that basket when it becomes difficult to carry.'[4]

So, while it's important to understand that you can indeed build a career out of your passion or passions, it's also crucial to realize that you may not necessarily be able to know those passions without some experimentation. Passion, it turns out, is often something you cultivate over time. And that is indeed very good news for those of us who don't possess that rare clarity about what we were born and meant to do from an early age itself.

For young people, especially, realizing that your passion isn't something you simply discover can relieve a tremendous amount of unnecessary stress and anxiety. If you are choosing an area of study for your undergraduate education, for example, but you're not clear about what you want to do yet, you don't need to feel like there's something wrong with you. You can make your best guess and then use your education to discover your passions, proclivities, interests and ambitions as you head further. It's similar when choosing your first job after college or graduate school. While you want to make sure you do your research and make the best choice possible, you also shouldn't overthink it. The average person will have many jobs in their life and while each of them may not particularly be a perfect fit, you can learn a lot from each of them.

The second core principle I want you to keep in mind as you go through the book is that passions are something you develop over time and not just something you discover. And this leads us to the next principle.

SIDEBAR: Indians Change Jobs More Than People in Other Countries

While the trend towards changing jobs several times throughout one's life is certainly global, it turns out that it's more extreme in India than anywhere else in the world. According to a 2019 Randstad Workmonitor Report, Indians had the highest rate of job change (67 per cent) among all countries.[5] In a similar 2015 study, 82 per cent of employees say that they plan to change jobs within the next twelve months[6]. Ironically, the Randstad study also found that Indians have the highest job satisfaction rating in the world (89 per cent were satisfied). So why are so many Indians changing jobs if they are so satisfied with their work?

One of the key factors driving job change in India (and abroad) is the desire to make more money. When you jump from one job to another, there is a greater opportunity to secure a better salary than receiving a raise within the same position. In addition to increased salaries, switching jobs also lends people the opportunity to advance in their industries or even within their own companies. Indians have a reputation for being some of the most ambitious and growth-oriented people in the world and it is likely that the high rate of job change is a reflection of this general mindset.

You Can Have Multiple Loves and Multiple Careers

In 1996, at thirty-two years old, I encountered an opportunity that would change my life forever. At the time, I was a manager at McKinsey & Company, and my professional life was heavily focused on business consulting. I loved my job and was very passionate about the various projects I was spearheading. As part of my work with McKinsey, I was tasked with consulting on the development of the Indian School of Business (ISB). One day, five years into the project, I got an offer that put me in a quandary.

After their initial choices to be the Founding Dean of ISB opted out, the Board approached me to take on the position for a year. I had little experience with education, so the thought of taking on such a big role, even though I was familiar with the project, was very intimidating to me. At the same time, I was afraid that taking a sabbatical from McKinsey would slow down my career as a partner. But in spite of my doubts, I was intrigued. The opportunity sparked a curiosity within me. After much deliberation and encouragement from a trusted mentor, I decided to take the leap and become ISB's Founding Dean.

Thus began what ended up being a long career in the world of education. While I didn't completely leave my work in the field of business behind, my newfound passion eventually led me to co-found one of India's top universities, Ashoka University and an online education company, Harappa Education. It has been a long and fulfilling journey and one that I would have never started had I not been willing to follow a new and fledgling passion for education and institution building all those years ago.

My own personal experience and those of countless others I've encountered over the years, has solidified my conviction that none of us are limited to just one passion—or one career—in our lives. As human beings, we are much more complex than we often realize. Society often tells us that we should be one thing, pursue one career, have one identity. And there are reasons for that. But as Walt Whitman once elegantly wrote in his famous poem *Song of Myself*, '(We) contain multitudes.' Within each of us, there is not just a banker or an engineer or a coach. There can be much, much more.

Like one of the people interviewed for this book, Anita Mackenzie, there can be an engineer and an international development specialist and an interior designer. Like Paroma Roy Chowdhury, there can be a journalist and an executive. Or like Smridhi Marwah, there can be a biomedical scientist, a non-profit communications director and an expert in women's studies.

As we round out the three core principles that make up the foundation of this book, it's crucial for you to contemplate this important insight: You aren't just one thing. You can have many different passions and build many different careers out of them. Understanding this truth is what will allow you to really discover and develop what your own passion-based career might look like.

Exercises

Below are a series of exercises to help you explore the topic of this chapter: building a career out of something you love. None of these are required. They are questions meant to help you reflect on some of the key points in this chapter. Feel free to work through all of them, some of them, or none of them. They are tools you can use to help your own process of self-discovery.

1. In the beginning of this chapter, I shared a scene from *This Is Us* about three siblings, one of whom—Kate—was struggling to figure out what she wanted to do with her life. Whom do you relate to more: Kate or her brothers? In other words, do you feel like you have a clear sense of what to do with your life, have no idea at all or are somewhere in the middle?

2. Before reading this chapter, did you think about passion as something you discover once or something you can develop over time? Did this chapter change the way you think about the topic?

3. Write down three or four things you know you are passionate about. This could be anything from mathematics to robots to drawing. Are these interests that you could see becoming the foundation for a career? Why or why not?

4. What would you say are the biggest obstacles you see to pursuing your passions?

5. Think of three people in your life that you consider to be successful (however you define that). What was their career trajectory like? Have they built careers out of their passions? Have their careers been a straight line or squiggly ones?

6. Extra Credit: Interview one or more of them to help you better answer this question.

2

It All Starts with Self-Discovery

Monica Hariharan grew up in a privileged family in Madras. When she was young, she was given umpteen opportunities to explore and experiment, attending private schools, playing sports and pursuing creative hobbies. But when it came time to choose a path entering 11th grade, she began to feel a familial and social pressure felt by many young Indians. She could choose to focus on either science or commerce. And according to old-school thinking, she could pursue a career as a doctor, an engineer or a businessperson.

Like so many young people, Monica wasn't sure about exactly what she wanted to do with her life at that critical juncture. She was only sixteen after all, with little life experience and so her view of what was possible was shaped primarily by the people and the culture around her. She came from a family of doctors and engineers, so despite the fact that she had little interest in math or science, she opted for the science track.

Fortunately for Monica, she had always been a bit of a rebel. While she did opt for a science major in high school and eventually university, she never intended to pursue a more traditional career as a doctor or engineer. Although her vision for her life was unclear, she did know a couple of things about her future career path; it had to be fun and it had to make a meaningful impact on the world. This passion eventually led her to make her first pivot, enrolling in journalism school; and then eventually to participate in the Young India Fellowship (YIF) at Ashoka University, which is where I met her.

The YIF is an interdisciplinary programme in liberal studies that I helped to start in order to encourage young people to develop skills and experiences that will empower them to become agents of change. It was perfect for Monica, because she knew she wanted to make a difference; she just didn't know how. And it was through her experience at YIF that she was presented with the framework to gain more clarity about who she was, what she was good at and what she wanted to do with her life. It allowed her the space to discover herself.

An Ongoing Process of Self-Discovery

Self-discovery, it turns out, is a crucial element to building a squiggly career. Like Monica, every single one of the people interviewed for the book cited this ability to understand who they were, what they were good at and what they wanted to do with their lives as foundational to their success. Like a 'North Star' for their career journeys, self-understanding served as a kind of guiding light that perpetually kept them on track.

But unlike the North Star, which is a fixed point in the sky, self-understanding for most of us, including most interviewees, is always changing. It's something you don't just do once when you're young. Sometimes it can take the form of a startling epiphany where you discover something fundamental about yourself that then shapes the rest of your life. At other times it can be more gradual and reflective, where you find that over time you develop and uncover passions and abilities you never knew you had before. Self-discovery is something you never stop undergoing. It's an ever-evolving process.

For Monica, self-discovery began when she was young, but it grew from there. She always knew that she wanted to do something meaningful and fun, but she didn't know what that meant. It took time for her to discover what 'fun and meaningful' looked like for her. When I first met her at YIF, for example, Monica was convinced that doing something meaningful had to look a certain way. 'Meaningful' for her meant doing something for the greater good, so she had considered working for non-profits addressing poverty, or a career in investigative journalism or even serving in the Indian Army.

But during her time at YIF, she learned that doing something meaningful could be much broader and more diverse than she had ever imagined. A meaningful career didn't necessarily need to take a more traditional form, like social activism. It could include business or the arts or even food. That experience led her to make her next pivot into the world of business. She took a position at a consulting firm, and eventually went back to school to get an MBA at Oxford University.

Monica, now thirty-one, is still very much in the midst of her process of self-discovery. She currently works at a UK-based food delivery start-up after a stint at a sports marketing firm. She is discovering her passion and talent for the world of business that she never knew she had all those years ago in high school, when she was first presented with choosing her life's path. And she's still continuing to have fun.

You Can't Force It

Human beings tend to naturally possess a difficulty with the unknown. We plan, strategize and manipulate outcomes to be more predictable. It is a deeply human characteristic that has allowed us to build vast civilizations with unparalleled technological capacities. Our desire to make the unknown known has led to advances in modern medicine, brought us to space and to explore the depths of the human psyche and soul. It is, all in all, a positive quality.

The desire to limit what we don't know can, however, create problems, especially when it comes to the process of self-discovery. It turns out that the complicated and subtle endeavours to find our passions, tap into our strengths and become aware of our weaknesses is not something you can necessarily plan out in advance or force to take place. It moves more organically than mechanically and for the most part is a process that moves according to its own pace.

But that doesn't mean we haven't tried. For decades, educational and corporate institutions have used psychometric assessments to help people at all stages of their careers with the process of self-discovery and figure out what professions they might be best suited for. One of the most popular assessments is the Myers-Briggs test, which consists of ninety-three different questions that, based on your answers, will generate not only a personalized psychological profile, but also generate a list of careers you might be best suited for. But despite the fact that over 2.5 million people take the Myers-Briggs test every year and it is used by eighty-nine of the *Fortune* 100 companies, there is a growing body of research undermining its validity and effectiveness. Not only have researchers found the test to be based on dubious psychological claims, but the actual results have been far from impressive and the insights and career suggestions generated by Myers-Briggs don't end up being all that useful to those who take it.[1]

Many of the critiques of Myers-Briggs and other psychometric assessments revolve around the fact that they tend to be overly reductionist. With Myers-Briggs, for example, you are categorized into a specific personality type based on your answers. And within that categorization, there is an implicit assumption that people tend to be one thing or another: introverted or extroverted, right-brained or left-brained, artistic or logical, interested in humanities or more scientifically minded.

But we all know that human beings just aren't that simple, or binary. It's possible for each of us to have strengths in two seemingly contradictory categories. None of us are only defined by one thing. And what we are good at and what we are passionate about can change over time. The late Steve Jobs, for example, wasn't just a tech genius. He studied calligraphy during his college years and credits that artistic background with helping him to refine Apple's now-legendary aesthetic. Or take Carly Fiorina, the former CEO of Hewlett-Packard. Before becoming the head of one of the world's largest tech companies, she majored in philosophy and medieval studies at Stanford University.

On one hand, this might seem like bad news. Wouldn't it be great to be able to simply take a test that would give you a deep and clear sense of who you are and what career would provide you the best chance for happiness and success? Like so many other elements of our world, creating systems and processes to help us better understand ourselves seems like something we should want, right?

But on the other hand, should something as important and profound as self-discovery be something you can simply reduce to a test or a formula? We are not robots after all. Our personalities aren't scripts or algorithms. Likewise, the process of discovering ourselves can't be robotic. It requires patience, trial and error and most of all, time. And this is the key point. As all of the people interviewed for this book can attest, you simply can't figure this out in advance. You have to go about the business of working and living to learn who you really are. You can't know how you respond under pressure, for example, until you experience real-world pressure. You can't know your working style until you spend time working in different professional environments. You'll never know your strengths and weaknesses as a manager until you find yourself in a situation where you are required to manage others.

So, when it comes to self-discovery, it's a mix of good news and bad news. The bad news is that there's no silver bullet. You just have to get your hands dirty. The good news is, there is probably much more talent, passion and capacity within you than you could ever imagine in advance. And you have your whole life to discover and unravel it.

Resisting the Pressure

If self-discovery can't be rushed, then why do we try so desperately to force it? Besides the natural human tendency to reduce the unknowns in our lives, a big source of pressure is society. It was remarkable to me how many of the people I interviewed for the book had a similar story. Like Monica, they were forced to choose an area of specialization at a young age and then stick to it. If they weren't sure what they wanted to do, they didn't want to admit it for fear of people thinking that something was wrong with them. As Monica pointed out, she looked around at her peers and they seemed to have it all figured out, so she thought she also needed to do the same. But ironically, most if not all of them probably felt the same way about her.

So where does all this pressure come from? The Indian educational system is one of the most competitive in the world and parents feel a tremendous amount of pressure for their children to succeed—pressure that they, in turn, apply to their kids.

Unfortunately, all of this pressure usually translates into what I call premature conformity. Students who are looking to get ahead often fall victim to the misguided assumption that by choosing a specialization early, they'll have an advantage. The sooner you decide to be an engineer, they think, the quicker you will reach a point of success. And in order to choose a career path quickly, students often force themselves to figure out who they are and what they want to do with their lives before they've had any real professional or life experience to base that decision on. The result, more often than not, is that they either choose the wrong path and end up limited in how far they can go in the long run, or they jump tracks at some point down the line. Monica, for example, chose engineering because that seemed like the easiest choice, but eventually abandoned it for a career path that was more suited to who she was.

Sadly, there is little indication that this culturally induced pressure is going away any time soon. In this high-pressure environment, young people need to find the resolve to resist forcing themselves to prematurely figure it all out. Like Monica, they need to find a way to make an initial choice without it being one that will bind them to a certain destiny for the rest of their lives. In an ideal world, their parents and mentors would support this more gradual approach to self-discovery. But this may not always be the case.

That's one of the reasons why I wrote this book. I want young people and their parents to understand that it's okay if you don't know what you want to do right up front. I want to help alleviate this pressure, from within and without, so that people can discover their passions, their strengths and their weaknesses more organically. I have found that this is the only way it really works in the long run.

SIDEBAR: Indian Students Globally among the Most Well-Rounded

Indian students are globally known for their fierce dedication to academics. According to Cambridge International's 2018 Global Education Census, students from India and China take more extra classes than any other country, primarily in chemistry, physics and math. But the same study also suggests that Indian students are among the most well-rounded in the world. According to the census, 72 per cent of Indian students participate in extracurricular activities, the highest rate of any country. The most popular activities, according to the census, are debating (36 per cent), science club (28 per cent), art (25 per cent), and book club (22 per cent). Indian students are also quite physically active. The Cambridge census found that 74 per cent of students play sports regularly, with badminton (37 per cent), football (30 per cent) and cricket (30 per cent) being the most popular.[2]

Discovering What You're Good (and Not So Good) At

When I first met Siya Sood, she was in the Vedica Scholars Programme for Women, which I co-founded

with Anuradha Das Mathur to offer young women a
postgraduate opportunity to prepare themselves for
leadership in the professional world. Siya was a student
in the programme, and still very much in the process of
figuring out what she wanted to do with her life.

Growing up, Siya had always been extremely bright,
but she had never really taken her education that seriously.
She came from a privileged family and had attended elite
boarding schools, but she was a self-described 'bad kid'
and never really applied herself. In college, she continued
the trend, choosing a large school where she could have
fun and party and majored in history, even though she
didn't really have a passion for it.

By the time she graduated from college, reality started
to set in for her. It was time to grow up, get serious and
figure out what she wanted to do with the rest of her life.
The problem was, she didn't really know what she was
good at, because she'd never really been in a position to
challenge herself.

While the Vedica Scholars Programme certainly
helped Siya to begin to develop some clarity about her
future, it wasn't until her first job where she truly started
the process of self-discovery. This was a theme for many
of the interviewees. They needed real-world experience
to really test themselves and discover their passions,
strengths and weaknesses. They needed the challenge of
work to bring their abilities into stark relief.

For Siya, her first real-world opportunity was with
the Albright Stonebridge Group (ASG), where she worked
very closely in a small group that included myself and
some other senior managers. Our main focus at ASG was

to help foreign companies across a wide variety of sectors, from defence and pharmaceuticals to technology and national security, to grow their operations in the country. As she was working so closely with senior members of the company, there was a steep learning curve. And this is exactly what someone like Siya needed to thrive. As she described it in our interview, it was the first time in her life where she felt truly challenged. And that brought out the best in her.

Whereas her traditional educational experience, while valuable, had focused primarily on grades and narrow metrics, her work at ASG focused more on results. Rather than her work being 'graded' like it was in school, she saw the real-time results of her efforts in the projects she was responsible for. If she was particularly thorough on a report for one of our clients, they would express gratitude for the usable data she gave them. That created a kind of instantaneous feedback loop that helped supercharge her professional development.

Through her work at ASG, Siya realized that she had two strengths in particular: interpersonal relations and communications. She had a knack for working collaboratively in teams, which is so crucial to most professions in the modern workplace and being sensitive to the needs of a wide variety of stakeholders. And she realized that she was very good at communicating complex subjects via diverse written and verbal mediums. As we will discuss in a later chapter, both of these are considered to be 'deeper' skills in that they transcend any particular job, industry, or profession. Unlike learning a technical skill, capacities like interpersonal relations and communication can be applied to virtually any career.

For Siya, discovering her strengths was deeply empowering. Neither was a surprise, as she had always been a people's person and a good communicator. But it wasn't until she put herself to the test in a professional environment that she learned the true value of her inherent talents. She was then able to leverage those strengths into a vibrant career that took her from ASG to a competitive job with McKinsey and eventually to a senior strategy position at an online education company.

That's the power of getting clear about who you are, what you want to do and what you're good at. Armed with that self-knowledge, you can find yourself in jobs and industries you never would have imagined yourself in. You can achieve levels of success that you didn't even think possible. And you can do it by simply being who you are.

Before we conclude our inquiry into discovering your strengths, I want to touch upon the opposite: understanding your weaknesses. I don't want to dwell on this aspect of self-knowledge too much, precisely because I find that we, as human beings and as a society, tend to focus too much on weaknesses and not enough on our strengths. There has been a tremendous amount of work done in the field of positive psychology to show that it's better not to get too caught up on what you're not good at; and focus more on how you can leverage the things you are good at.

That being said, no conversation about self-discovery is complete without understanding the areas where you need improvement. And like your strengths, your weaknesses are most often discovered through direct experience. For Siya, she discovered that one of her weaknesses was her work ethic. After a lifetime of doing just enough to get by, the demands of her first job at ASG was a real wake-up call for her. She soon realized that she had to develop new habits of hard work and dedication that she had never been able to cultivate before. Of course, it didn't take her long to figure it out, but she needed to discover this weakness for herself in order to evolve.

The same can be said for your aversions, which are the opposite of your passions. While it's arguably more important to figure out what you're passionate about, you also need to know what you don't like to do. And just like every other dimension of self-discovery, this is something that takes time and experience. With Monica, for example, she initially thought that journalism would be a great avenue for her to do something meaningful, but after studying it she soon realized that she didn't really enjoy the work. Siya, too, discovered what she didn't want to do through her first two jobs. After two positions in the world of business consulting, she eventually realized that she was more passionate in the world of education and pivoted into that field. She is now back at McKinsey working on leadership development, taking her interest in education to a whole new level.

In all these cases, the key to self-discovery is real-world experience. You just can't do it in a vacuum. You have to test yourself in order to discover yourself. Like Siya and Monica, you need to get your hands dirty in the real working world to figure out what aspects of who you are might be valuable to the development of your career.

Self-Discovery Is a Lifelong Journey

One of the most important lessons I gleaned from my interviews for this book was the fact that there is no one common path for self-discovery. For some of us, we become clear about what we want to do and what we're good at when young. Srikant Sastri, for example, knew from a very young age that he wanted to be an entrepreneur. He held on to that vision and successfully started multiple companies throughout his career. Others, like Monica and Siya, left school with little idea about what they wanted to do or what they were good at, but figured it out through experience (and are still figuring it out even today). So regardless of where you are in your journey, it's crucial that you don't feel like you're not doing it right. Self-discovery is unique for each person.

Of all the people I interviewed for the book, Anita Mackenzie's path to self-discovery may be the most long and winding one. Anita is the founder of a Singapore-based home styling company called Plum Chutney, but it took her thirty years to discover her passion for interior design and build a career out of it. Her career, it turns out, represents one of the key insights about the process of self-discovery: it isn't something that happens just once or twice; it's a lifelong journey of introspection, trial and error, coupled with perpetual growth.

Anita comes from an older generation where the pathways to success were much narrower than they are today and the early part of her career reflected just that. She was raised in a progressive family in Patna where she and her two sisters were always told they could do and be anything they wanted, which was rare for that era. That said, there were still a few options for her when it came to education and she chose to take a STEM path in her high school and undergraduate education and an MBA at the prestigious Indian Institute of Management in Ahmedabad.

When she finished her MBA, Anita began the first phase of her career, working for Unilever, which has had a huge presence in India for decades. For Anita, like many professionals, much of her growth came within her long tenure with Unilever, as opposed to moving between multiple companies. Unilever wants its new employees to have a direct experience of the 'real India' by working in sales. Anita followed suit, spending several years gaining invaluable experience selling a variety of Unilever products to the diverse cultures of India. It was during this time that she made her first self-discovery: marketing and branding.

Anita spent the next five years working in this sector of the company and learned a tremendous amount along the way. In particular, she discovered and cultivated both a talent for holding 'the big picture' while diving deep into the nitty-gritties of any given project or problem. This turned out to be a key skill that helped her in marketing management, but also served her throughout the rest of her career. And while

Anita attributes some of this skill development to her MBA training, she didn't really learn to apply it until she was working within the complex and demanding environment of Unilever.

After a decade of working in marketing and branding, Anita was presented with an opportunity that would define the next phase of her career and with it she uncovered a whole new dimension to herself. She had been wanting to do more international work and it just so happened that Unilever presented her an opportunity to become one of Prince Charles' private secretaries. Unilever is a global leader in corporate social responsibility (CSR) and this position was a kind of partnership between the company and the Prince of Wales's office to help manage his charitable initiatives in the UK and globally. In her role, Anita was responsible for the activities within the British Commonwealth, with a special focus on India.

As Anita puts it, she grew tremendously during those years. Being outside of her comfort zone—living in the UK and stepping out of the traditional corporate world—allowed her to find new interests and capacities she never knew she possessed. She developed a passion for social responsibility and increased her multicultural understanding as well. Once she finished her stint at the Prince of Wales office she got a chance to apply those back in Unilever, spearheading a programme to induct social and environmental responsibility into the heart of their Global Brands. Having met her future husband Alistair in Britain and now part of the Indian diaspora in the UK, she also developed a particular interest in the intersection of those two cultures.

And this is what led to the final (for now) phase of her career—a pivot that seemingly came out of left field, but that actually brought together many of the skills and interests she'd been cultivating throughout her career. Anita had always had a personal passion for interior design and at this juncture she felt a strong calling to start something that was entirely her own—a venture that would allow her to exercise her creative talents while also expressing her unique personality as an Indian who had adopted Britain as her home. She earned a Diploma in interior design from Nottingham Design Academy and started her own online home decor store. That's how Plum Chutney was born.

The name 'Plum Chutney' is an homage to the Indian and British cultures that shaped her. It started out as an online store that sold home ware and accessories inspired by India's many charms but designed through the lens of Britain's more quirky interior aesthetic. Plum Chutney was part of a growing cohort of inventive online retail stores that were challenging traditional British brick and mortar businesses through innovative design. She drew upon her marketing and branding experience to build a strong brand for Plum Chutney and a thriving retail and online retail business. She was also able to tap into her passion for social responsibility by creating a venture where the goods she sold in the store were designed in India and then sold in the UK, providing opportunities for designers and producers in her home country.

During the seven years of running Plum Chutney in the UK, Anita was primarily focused on online sales, but also did home interior design consultations for select customers. Then in 2019, her husband got a job in Singapore and the family moved. She decided to close the online business and evolve Plum Chutney into an interior design company for Singapore-based clients. The beauty of this shift for Anita was that she could take the Plum Chutney brand she had cultivated through her retail venture and apply it directly to her new interior design focus. She is now applying to her clients' homes the perfect blend of her British (Plum) and Indian (Chutney) aesthetic that helped build her successful retail business.

Anita's story inspires me. She has shown, through her own career, that you can continue to grow, change and learn new things about yourself all throughout your life and career. The young engineering student who turned an MBA into a career in corporate marketing and branding, then shifted into global non-profit management and eventually into interior design is living proof that self-learning is a continuous process and that none of us are simply good at only one thing.

While Anita admits that she wishes she had the opportunity to discover and cultivate her creative talents in the beginning of her career, she doesn't consider any of her professional experiences to be wrong turns or implausible. Each unlocked something new in Anita and built towards the next chapter of her career. This is the beauty of self-discovery. It is a never-ending process. You will keep discovering things about yourself as long as you continue to be engaged in the process of inquiry.

SIDEBAR: A Leader in Corporate Social Responsibility

Unilever is known globally as a leader in the emerging field of corporate social responsibility (CSR). For decades, the company has invested significant energy and resources in both social and environmental sustainability. And they started doing it long before CSR became a trend.

But for Unilever, CSR isn't just about charity or improving their company's reputation amongst an increasingly conscious audience of consumers. It's built into the bottom line of their business. They have found through many product campaigns throughout the developing world that their business does better when it is taking responsibility for the sustainability of the communities they work with.

For example, one of Unilever's bestselling products is Lifebuoy antibacterial soap, which is prolific throughout rural India. Alongside the promotion of the product, Unilever has also invested in significant public service campaigns to educate the public about the value of handwashing. They funded clinical trials to show the positive effects of handwashing on public health and partnered with the World Health Organization (WHO) to spread the word throughout India's vast network of rural villages.

As a result of Unilever's efforts, they were able to have a significant impact on India's public health. But their motives weren't purely altruistic. The increased value on handwashing amongst their target demographic also dramatically expanded the market for Unilever's Lifebuoy soap. While it certainly falls into the category of a corporate social responsibility, the Lifebuoy campaign was really more an example of grassroot marketing.

Exercises

The exercises below are designed to help you get to know yourself better, not like a psychometric assessment, but more of a reflection based on what you know today. None of the exercises are mandatory. You can skip around, pick and choose, or if you don't find them useful, skip them altogether.

1. Think of a situation where you were given advice about what career you should pursue. This could be from a parent, a teacher or a peer. Did you agree or disagree with their advice? Over time, has it been proven to be accurate or not?
2. Do a pressure-free, judgment-free self-assessment: What are four to five of your key strengths? What are four to five qualities or skills that you need to work on? Is there anything specific that you want to cultivate or change in order to accomplish your goals?
3. Get feedback from a trusted mentor or friend about what they perceive to be your key strengths and weaknesses. Compare them to your own assessment. What were the differences and did any of them surprise you? Why or why not?
4. Think about two qualities or capacities you have that might seem like an odd pairing. For example, you might love both mathematics and art. Or you might

be a talented violin player and athlete. How does this pairing of qualities make you unique?

5. Write a brief, three to four sentence personal statement about who you are. This shouldn't be overly formal, like something you'd put in a job application or LinkedIn profile. Focus more on your deeper qualities and passions. What have you learnt about yourself over the course of your life?

6. Extra Credit: Save this statement so you can revisit and revise it once a year.

3

Balancing Breadth and Depth

One of the most thought-provoking books I've read over the past few years was the *New York Times* bestseller by the American sportswriter, David Epstein, *Range: Why Generalists Triumph in a Specialized World*. Epstein—a former journalist for *Sports Illustrated* magazine and author of *The Sports Gene*—challenges the modern assumption that, in order to thrive in one's vocation, it's necessary to specialize in it as early as possible. He starts in the world of sports, citing the careers of tennis legend Roger Federer and various members of the US Women's Olympic gold-medallist soccer team as examples of athletes who benefited significantly from playing a wide variety of sports early in their lives before eventually choosing one to focus on. He then expands his thesis far beyond athletics into the realm of business, arts and education. He makes a strong and well-researched case that those who succeed in the long run are the ones who develop a wide range of skills and experiences, especially early in their lives, that they can apply to the rest of their career, even if it ends up being a narrow field.

The book, for me, sparked a kind of epiphany. None of Epstein's insights were necessarily new. Quite to the contrary. I have always been a generalist myself and touted the virtues of having a well-balanced approach to education and professional development. My background includes everything from robotic engineering to business consulting to educational entrepreneurship. But Epstein takes this insight to a whole new level, powerfully articulating a perspective that I've held quietly for much of my career and then backs it up with a wealth of research, data and case studies.

It turns out that being a generalist—in your skills, your education and your life experiences—is the most effective approach to achieving long-term success in even the narrowest of disciplines. But in our world of hyper-specialization, trumpeting the path of the generalist might seem naive at best or heresy at worst. So much of our world is geared towards finding your focus early and then doubling down on it in order to get ahead. Our educational system forces young people to choose a path as teenagers and often emphasizes the rote learning of ephemeral skills and information rather than more profound capacities that will serve them best in the long run.

With all this pressure to specialize, it can often feel like a Herculean task to go in the other direction. And yet all of the people I interviewed for the book were, in their own ways, generalists. Some took a liberal arts approach to their education. Others experimented with different jobs to develop a variety of experiences that they incorporated into their long-term careers. All of them, in one way or another, were able to develop a diversity of 'deeper skills' that transcended any particular job or discipline and then apply those skills in unexpected ways throughout their careers.

Don't get me wrong. I'm not against specialization and neither is anyone who I interviewed for the book. In fact, I believe that we all need to find at least one area of our professional lives that we specialize in. But in my experience, specialization is something we need to grow into as we evolve, both personally and professionally. It can't be forced. Nor should it come at the expense of learning a broad range of skills. Specializing in a discipline is, in my view, a skill in and of itself. Learning how to become a master at something, whether it be an approach to management, a coding language or writing book proposals, is a capacity we all need to develop.

The key is to find that balance of breadth and depth. Of variety and focus. Of being a generalist and a specialist. Of specific skill sets and deeper, more universal skills. That's what this chapter is all about. We're going to explore how to achieve this balance of breadth and depth. We'll draw on the experiences of many of the people I interviewed and discover how they have been able to strike this balance in their own lives and careers. We'll talk about what educational approach you should take to develop this balance. Finally, we'll talk about the value of specialization and why learning *how* to specialize might be even more important than the areas you choose to specialize in.

Choosing Your Educational Path

One of the most common questions I get from young people and their parents is around their educational choices. In particular, people want to know both what and where they should study. And this doesn't just come from people entering college. It also applies to those deciding what to do for their graduate education.

As we have been discussing thus far in this chapter, developing a balance of breadth and depth in your capacities is crucial for long-term success. And specializing at the expense of cultivating a broad range of skills can often inhibit your progress. So, if we are aiming to balance both breadth and depth in our capacities, which educational path is best? Especially in a society that pressurizes us into making these choices at ever-younger ages?

Of course, I have no simple answer to this question. There just isn't one be-all, end-all solution to the issue. Each one of us is different. We have different backgrounds, goals, strengths and capacities. There's no one best way to pursue your education.

That being said, there are some important lessons I've gleaned from my own professional career, from working in the world of education for decades and speaking with many of the interviewees for this book. None of these lessons are prescriptive. They aren't any black-and-white rules that you must follow to succeed. These are more general guidelines and perspectives to keep in mind as you choose an educational path for yourself:

1. You don't have to know (yet).

2. The institution matters more than your major.
3. A liberal arts-style education generally serves you best in the long run.

Let's explore each of these in more depth.

You Don't Have to Know (Yet)

As we've discussed in the opening chapters to this book, there is a tremendous amount of pressure to make the 'right' choices about your education and career in order to have a successful future. As a result, many young people feel like they need to figure out exactly the right institution to attend and the perfect major to focus on. But as I've argued, this kind of pressure doesn't really help young people, nor does it reflect the reality of the world we're living in. This is especially the case around your educational choices. The world is changing so fast, that it's very difficult to predict what skills or capacities would be relevant in the future. And many of the valuable lessons you glean in your life will happen along the way. You simply can't perfectly prepare for the world we're living in.

So, the first lesson to keep in mind as you make your educational choices is that it's okay to not know what the best path is. In fact, there is probably not a perfectly correct choice for you—and that's fine. It might seem contradictory for my primary piece of advice about choosing an educational path to be, that it doesn't matter as much as you think it does. But I'm doing this for a reason. Don't get me wrong, your education is important—extremely important. It will often set the tone for the rest of your career and give you some foundational skills and experiences that you will draw on for the rest of your life. It's just that adding extra pressure to the situation won't help you in the long run.

If you can't figure out what you want to study or find a clear-cut number one choice for your undergraduate or graduate education, it's okay.

The Institution Is More Important Than the Major

One of the most common insights that the interviewees for this book shared was that what they chose to major in during school didn't matter nearly as much as the school they attended. Whether they were reflecting back from the mid-point or the end of their careers, nearly everyone de-emphasized their area of academic focus. Many didn't use their major at all after graduation. But everyone emphasized that they were glad they had chosen their respective school.

This is a particularly important point for many young people who are choosing an educational path, because many will choose an institution based on whether or not they have a good programme in their chosen area of study. Of course, this can be a good move if you are already clear about the path you want to take. But most of us, whether we know it or not, aren't that clear about what we want to do with our lives. And so, it's a better strategy to focus on finding the right school, regardless of what specific disciplines they focus on.

There are a few reasons for this. Firstly, the reputation of the school you attend can open all kinds of doors for you in the future. Siya Sood, who we met in the last chapter, said that one of the best decisions she made was to attend Lady Sri Ram College for Women, which is a renowned school. She credits the reputation of the school for helping her get future jobs, graduate school opportunities and make connections. The specific school may not matter as much as going to a school with a good reputation. In other words, as long as you get into a good school, it doesn't matter which one.

The other primary reason that school matters has more to do with culture. For example, if you grew up in a rural environment and want to challenge yourself to grow by immersing yourself in a more cosmopolitan environment, you might choose an urban school. Or if you prefer to be in a setting with a wider variety of people, you could attend a larger university rather than a small private college. This 'cultural' fit is often overlooked by young people when they think about where they want to go to school, but it is often cited by people midway through their careers as one of the most crucial elements of their education.

Finally, it's important to choose a school that will give you more opportunities to grow in diverse ways. If you're in a richer academic environment, you're more likely to be challenged and therefore grow. As we'll discuss in the next section, a liberal arts education might be best for that; but gaining a liberal-arts-like experience can also happen at a more technical school.

In Defence of the Liberal Arts

Nikhil Sud is rare among his peers as he knew from a young age itself that he wanted to pursue a liberal arts education, rather than the more specialized degree programmes emphasized in most Indian preparatory schools. Born and raised in New Delhi in a family that put a high value on education, Nikhil excelled in school, but was turned off by the often-myopic focus of many around him. He recalls a common conversation during his pre-university years where his friends would ask him, 'What engineering training program have you enrolled in?' And while he did feel the pressure to choose a more traditional, narrow lane, Nikhil ultimately chose a more broad-based education where he could take a variety of classes.

What is a liberal arts education? A simple definition would be a curriculum that includes classes across a wide variety of subjects from four general sectors: the arts, humanities, social and physical sciences. The main goal behind studying the liberal arts is not to learn a specific skill or area of study, though most students still choose a primary area of focus. Rather, a liberal arts education is aimed at cultivating an ability to think critically across disciplines and to see the interconnections between them. As the National Educational Policy 2020 states, 'The very idea that all branches of creative human endeavour, including mathematics, science, vocational subjects, professional subjects, and soft skills should be considered 'arts', has distinctly Indian origins. This notion of a 'knowledge of many arts' or what in modern times is often called the 'liberal arts' (i.e., a liberal notion of the arts) must be brought back to Indian education, as it is exactly the kind of education that will be required for the 21st century.'[1] Or as Nikhil put it, he pursued a liberal arts education because he wanted to develop what he believes is the most important capacity of all: the ability to think.

At that time, Nikhil was not excited by the options for a liberal arts education in India. There are certainly a growing number of such schools in the country, including Ashoka University, but the liberal arts tradition remains much stronger abroad, especially in Europe, Canada and the United States. The lack of quality liberal arts institutions in India is, I believe, one of the main forces driving our country's 'brain drain', as many of our brightest young thinkers leave India for their education and a large percentage of them never come back. Like so many others, Nikhil decided to study abroad, enrolling in Yale University in New Haven, Connecticut.

During his time at Yale, Nikhil majored in economics, but took a wide variety of classes outside his discipline and was very involved in a number of extracurricular activities, like debating, which further enriched his educational experience. And while he eventually moved into a more specialized track, attending law school after his undergraduate work was complete, he credits his liberal arts degree with giving him a foundation that has served him throughout his law school years and career.

At this point, you might be asking a question that many students and their parents raise when confronted with the possibility of a liberal arts education. It goes something like this, 'Okay, I get that a liberal arts education can teach you how to think and make you more well-rounded, but can it actually get you a job?' Indeed, the liberal arts are often derided as philosophically interesting, but practically useless. And there are plenty of jokes about liberal arts graduates working in coffee shops because they don't have the skills to get a 'real job'. This is a big part of the reason that there is so much emphasis on a STEM curriculum in India and in many places around the world. Since so many of the available jobs are in the STEM fields, young people assume they should just focus on STEM training from an early age.

But while there may be a nugget of truth to this commonly-held belief, the general cultural bias towards more 'practical' degrees misses a much greater point about the value of a liberal arts (or liberal arts-inspired) education. As Nikhil pointed out, the core value of liberal arts is that it aims to cultivate a broad range of deeper skills with critical thinking as the foundation, which can be applied to more specialized skill sets later in your career. In fact, there is considerable evidence to suggest that a liberal arts foundation can end up being more practical and useful in the long run. There has been substantial research and media coverage in recent years about the 'skill gap' that many companies are experiencing among recent graduates entering the workforce. According to the India Skills Report 2021, less than half of the younger population (45.9 per cent) are considered employable.[2]

While there are several complex factors driving the skill gap, many have cited the narrow training that quite a number of our more technical institutions offer students. A recent study conducted by Stanford University in collaboration with HSE University Moscow and published in *Nature Human Behaviour* tracked 30,000 engineering students across India, Russia, China and the US throughout their four undergraduate years to monitor the development of their critical thinking skills. The study found that Indian engineering students (along with Russian and Chinese) significantly lagged behind their American counterparts when it came to critical thinking.[3]

In an article for the *Higher Education Review*, Mimi Roy, an associate professor at the Jindal School of Liberal Arts and Humanities, explains why she believes Indian students are falling behind. 'The pedagogy at most techno-institutions is not thought provoking and relies mostly on rote learning and exam-based lock step methods.' She then concludes, 'Without giving sufficient emphasis on the liberal education, we not only challenge the practical needs of the 21st century, but we also run the risk of our current and future generations not being able to understand the freedom of knowledge and the art of living happy.'[4]

SIDEBAR: Far from Home

Due to the relatively high quality of educational institutions beyond India's borders, Indian students have had a long tradition of going abroad for their undergraduate and postgraduate studies. And while there has been progress in establishing higher quality education options within the country, the study-abroad trend has been accelerating. According to research by the International Education Consultancy Abroad, the number of Indian students studying abroad grew from 66,000 a decade ago to over 7,50,000 in 2019, making India second to only China in terms of the number of students attending schools outside their borders.

According to IEC Abroad's research, there are several factors influencing this rise. Firstly, India's population is growing younger and there are simply far more college-aged students than there were a decade ago. Secondly, India's domestic institutions have become highly competitive, many of which accept only 1–2 per cent of their applicants. Finally, India has become far more integrated into the global economy and students are more familiar (and comfortable) with the countries they're studying in (the US, Canada and Australia are the top three) and feel that their prospects for securing a better-paying job will be higher if they attend a foreign university.[5]

The trend has continued even as the COVID-19 pandemic has made travel more difficult. A recent study by AECC Global found that while the overall number of students studying abroad decreased due to COVID-19 travel restrictions, 91 per cent of Indian students have a desire to study abroad once the pandemic is over.[6]

Diversifying Your Educational Experience

It may seem at this point that I am an unapologetic advocate for the liberal arts and would advise all young people to pursue that educational path. But it's not that simple. Attending a liberal arts college isn't the right choice for everyone, nor is it always an option. Some people know from an early age what they want to do and find a more specialized educational pathway to get them there. Others might not be able to afford a liberal arts education, as most institutions tend to be more elite. And as Nikhil discovered, there simply aren't as many liberal arts colleges in India and not everyone wants to go abroad for their education.

The good news is that it's possible to gain many of the benefits of a liberal arts education even if you don't attend a liberal arts college. Take Srikant Sastri for example, whom we'll meet in depth later in the book. He is part of my generation and came up in a time where there were really no liberal arts options for him to pursue as an undergraduate. He attended an engineering school and realized almost immediately that he didn't want to pursue an engineering career. So, he made the best of his academic experience by actively choosing diverse opportunities on campus. He got involved in extracurricular activities like the student government, which not only allowed him to develop new and diverse skill sets, but also helped connect him to a wider network of peers and mentors.

I had a similar experience during my graduate education at the University of Pennsylvania. Though Penn was a liberal arts university, I was engaged in a very focused course of study: mechanical engineering. It would have been easy for me to keep my blinders on and focus entirely on my area of study. But I made a point to take many classes in areas like computer science that were outside my immediate discipline. There was no real practical 'reason' to take these classes, beyond my own curiosity and yet they ended up being some of the most pivotal highlights of my education. I made it a point to attend talks and events in literature and the arts, inspired by my childhood exposure to Hindi literature and Hindustani Classical music. I was exposed to brilliant professors and students from completely different fields than my own and that broadened my view of the world. I ended up doing a PhD in Robotics, with a thesis supervisory committee that had a mechanical engineer, a material scientist, a computer scientist and psychologist.

This is the key point. Regardless of what kind of school you choose to attend, it's crucial that you actively seek out a diversity of experiences, individuals and classes. This is true for those who attend liberal arts schools, or engineering schools like Srikant did. While your undergraduate education is certainly meant to give you foundational knowledge in whichever major you choose, it's about much more than that. It's one of the best opportunities you'll have in your life to experiment and explore. You will be surrounded by so many different kinds of people with different life experiences and areas of expertise. The more you take advantage of this stimulating environment, the more well-rounded you will become and the more you'll set yourself up for success in the long run.

SIDEBAR: The STEM Advantage Fades Over Time

There has long been an assumption that the best way to secure a solid, high-paying job is to pursue training in Science, Technology, Engineering and Math, collectively known as STEM. And while this might be true in the short-term, new research suggests that the STEM advantage fades as workers get deeper into their careers. In a 2019 *New York Times* article, 'In the Salary Race, Engineers Spring but English Majors Endure,' David Deming shares a variety of compelling statistics showing that students with STEM degrees earn more than humanities majors in their early jobs, but the gap closes and in some cases, flips as they get deeper into their careers.[7]

For example, Deming cites the US Census Bureau American Community Survey to show that individuals aged twenty-three to twenty-five with degrees in computer science and engineering earned on average 37 per cent more than those who majored in history or social sciences. But by the age of forty, those with history and social science degrees were actually out-earning the STEM majors.[8]

Deming, who is the director of the Malcolm Wiener Center for Social Policy at the Harvard Kennedy School, attributes this phenomenon to several factors. First off, there are a greater number of tech jobs in the market and so recent graduates tend to be in higher demand. But there is also a higher turnover in STEM careers, because the required skill sets evolve and change rapidly. This means that while a STEM education is a solid foundation for your career, you need to constantly learn new skills to keep up. These changes don't occur as rapidly in more social-science-based careers. Finally, mid-career salaries tend to be highest in business and management positions and STEM graduates don't have an advantage in these areas.

So, while liberal arts degrees don't pay as well in the short run, they tend to support higher earnings in the long run. What's the lesson here? It's not that you shouldn't pursue a STEM-based education if you want to earn more money. STEM graduates have tremendous earning potential. The key insight is that the skills that will help you to advance in your career tend to be the 'soft skills' like we're exploring in this chapter. And these can be cultivated at any point in your education and career!

Learning *How* to Specialize

Nikhil might have as much passion for the liberal arts as any person I know. But he is also a firm believer that alongside the breadth that such an education provides, it's also important to gain the depth that comes from specializing in a particular field. For him, that came in the form of law school, which he attended at the same institution where he had pursued his undergraduate degree (Yale University).

He was attracted to law, not because he wanted to become a lawyer, but because he was compelled by the clarity of thinking that law requires. Again, for Nikhil critical thinking is the most foundational of all skills. Nikhil felt that because he had such a rich and diverse undergraduate experience, he was ready to move from breadth into depth by choosing one specific area to really dive into. And because he had such a strong and multidimensional background from his liberal arts education, he was able to pursue his law degree with far more perspective.

Nikhil is actually quite critical of a trend he's observed in some professionals: an over-embrace of 'generalism'. He argues that the mantra 'if you're smart, you can read a few articles on any topic and figure it out' is emphasized in many professional settings and is certainly helpful but has important limits that people often don't recognize. The more specialized a subject matter gets, the more important specialized training becomes. For example, he notes that being smart and reading a few articles on antitrust policy does not even remotely equip you to advise clients on it, but he sees so many people doing just that—to the detriment of everyone involved. No one wants to ride in a plane piloted by a very smart, well-read captain who hasn't logged thousands of hours in the cockpit.

The point is that while we shouldn't be too narrow in our approach, we should also avoid being too broad. We need to strike a balance between breadth and depth. In his book *Range*, David Epstein articulates a key insight into balancing breadth and depth. All of the people he profiled in the book as examples of individuals who pursued a range of sports, jobs, educational experiences and skills, all ended up eventually choosing one particular area where they excelled. This led him to articulate one of the key principles of developing range: generalize early, but specialize late. While it is important to have a diversity of skills, at some point, we all choose a specialty (sometimes even more than once).

I agree with Epstein's conclusion and it has borne out in my own career and those of others I've observed over the years. However, there is one twist that I would add to his insight. In my experience, the main benefit of going deeply into one discipline or skill or career is learning *how* to specialize. This, I have found, is a skill in and of itself and it's one that I have found extremely useful throughout my own career.

Completing a PhD in Robotics, for example, helped me to develop the rigour and focus that comes with such a degree. I had to become deeply familiar with the entire field—the latest research, industry trends, and the key individuals and institutions. Mastering this field gave me tremendous confidence in my ability to go all the way with something.

By learning how to specialize, I was prepared for the many other pivots I encountered in my career. When I was tasked with helping launch the Indian School of Business, for example, my specialization skills came in particularly handy. At the time, my background was in engineering and business consulting and I had no professional experience in the world of higher education. But because of my past specialization, I knew how to quickly learn what I needed to learn to perform my duties as the project leader and then the Founding Dean of the school. I was not an expert right off the bat, of course and I learned a lot on the job. But my ability to quickly master a new area of expertise allowed me to make what ended up being a dramatic career shift.

While all of the skills you master in your career will be important, none of them will be as important as the skill of learning to master them in the first place.

Striking Your Balance

I want to conclude this chapter with one more nugget from Epstein's book: 'Learning is most efficient in the long run when it is really inefficient in the short run.' While this can apply to so many dimensions of your educational journey, it may be most relevant for the kind of educational path you choose to go down.

Don't fall victim to the false belief that you need to pick a specialization early and then double down on it. Give yourself the time and space to experiment in your academic career by choosing an institution with diverse opportunities to pursue different topics and interests. Aim for balance, not expedience. Don't be afraid to take a longer and more winding path. It will benefit you in the long run.

Exercises

Below are a series of exercises you can use to help think through your educational journey. Don't worry, you don't have to complete the exercises if you don't want to. Feel free to do some or all of them and complete them in any order you wish.

1. Reflect on your own experience of thinking about your educational future. Do you feel pressure to choose a certain type of college or area of study? If so, where is that pressure coming from?
2. Thought exercise: If you could go anywhere for your undergraduate or graduate education, where would

it be? If you've already graduated, where would you have wanted to go if there were no limitations?

3. Make a list of some of your top college choices. Visit their websites and reflect on the 'culture' of each institution. Do any of them stand out more than others?

4. If you were to choose an area to specialize in today, what would it be? Has that changed over time?

5. Speak with a trusted mentor and ask them about their educational experience. Find out where they went to school, what they studied in, if they would have done anything differently etc.

4

Focusing on the Right Skills

These days, there is extensive discussion in both corporate and educational circles about skills. The overarching theme of these conversations is determining which skills are most important for long-term agility in the ever-shifting working world. Which skills are most important for young people to acquire for sustained success? What skills should educational institutions emphasize to better prepare students for the workforce? How can companies help to better assess and develop the important skill sets of their employees?

Many experienced people suggest that the key to staying agile is learning to anticipate and acquire the technical skills that will be most valuable in the future. The geeks and hackers who learned HTML code before most of us had even heard of the internet were suddenly in high demand when everyone wanted to create a website. But while getting ahead of the skill curve is a valuable and worthwhile pursuit, the truth is that it's just not enough. Learning a new technical skill might get you your next job, but what happens when things inevitably shift and you're required to adapt yet again?

This 'skill gap' is becoming a significant problem in the corporate world, as many companies are finding it difficult to find the talent and capacities they need within the current workforce. The 2018 India Skills Report found that 61 per cent of businesses across multiple sectors were experiencing a lack of talent within their organizations.[1] A similar survey conducted by The Adecco Group in 2019 found that 92 per cent of US-based executives think American workers aren't as skilled as they need to be. And that same study found that 44 per cent of executives cited 'soft' skills, like critical thinking, collaboration and communication, as those that are most lacking and in demand.

Given all of this confusion around necessary skills, I wanted to ask the people I interviewed for the book: which skills have been most important for their own careers? Their answers were both instructive and fascinating. They range from the ability to see the big picture to solid time management to the capacity to communicate effectively in multiple contexts. And while some of the skills that people cited were very specific, most were the kind of deep skills that cut across industries, jobs and cultures.

We'll spend this chapter exploring these essential skills. These are not meant to be prescriptive. Rather, I'm trying to give you a general sense of the kind of skills that tend to help you in the long run. Again, we're not talking about technical abilities. We're talking about the deeper qualities and capacities that you can use as foundational blocks for a successful career.

Transferable Skills for a Non-Linear World

Ambika Nigam is what you might call a workplace skills expert. After a successful career spanning finance, marketing and digital media, she decided to start an online career discovery company, Zeit, to help solve a problem that she had faced her whole career: how to find the right job for her unique skill set?

Like most people, she shifted jobs and industries multiple times throughout her career to that point. As she puts it, careers today are more like jungle gyms than ladders. Most people are constantly shifting positions and industries. And yet, most career discovery companies and professional networking platforms aren't really designed to support non-linear careers like hers.

With Zeit, Ambika helps people to assess themselves and figure out which of their skills are most transferable to the industries and jobs they're interested in and more importantly, how to communicate those skills to potential employers. As a result of her work, she's developed a sophisticated understanding of the kinds of skills that tend to be most transferable across industries and in-demand by employers.

I found my conversation with Ambika to be particularly edifying because many of the skills she identified overlapped with the skills I've identified in my work with Harappa Education. Harappa is an online education company I co-founded in 2018 to help individuals and companies to address their own skill gaps. We have identified five general categories of 'thrive skills' that tend to be important across industries:

1. Communication
2. Collaboration
3. Critical thinking
4. Problem-solving
5. Leadership

It turns out that we are not alone. Most of the skills that Ambika and the other interviewees for this book fell into these five categories and there has been substantial independent research pointing to similar conclusions. According to a 2018 survey by the National Association of Colleges and Employers, for example, the three attributes of college graduates that employers considered most important were written communication, problem-solving and the ability to work in a team.[2] Similarly, in the LinkedIn 2018 Workforce Report, leadership, communication, collaboration and time management are cited as the most in-demand soft skills.[3]

While no organizational structure can comprehensively cover every essential skill, these five tend to come close, so we will use them as the general structure for the rest of the chapter.

SIDEBAR: What You Can Do That a Machine Can't

Technology and innovation, while significant drivers of our global economic engine, have always had a love-hate relationship with the workforce. Why? In many situations, they make our work easier, safer and much more efficient. But on the other hand, automation has made and continues to make many jobs redundant, requiring workers to constantly upgrade their skill sets to keep up with the changing marketplace. Like a predator-prey cycle, automation puts pressure on the workforce to evolve and adapt as tasks that used to be performed by humans but are now taken over by computers, applications and machines.

But there is one domain that has remained relatively immune to automation's rapid advance: the area of capacities often referred to as 'soft' or 'social' skills. These capacities have proven difficult to replace with technology (though advances in artificial intelligence are becoming a threat) and include many of the skills we're exploring in this chapter: communication, emotional intelligence and leadership. According to a long-term economic analysis by the National Bureau of Economic Research, most of the job growth since 1980 has been within careers that require extensive social interaction. Jobs that include a high degree of analytical and mathematical processing, but relatively low levels of social interaction have declined. Similarly, the higher-paying jobs tend to be those that require the most social skills.[4]

What does this tell us about the future? As we venture forward into the 'brave new world' that awaits us all, it's crucial to develop these deeper skills that will resist the accelerating trend towards more and more automation. Otherwise, we'll eventually end up being outpaced by machines!

Communication

The ability to communicate effectively was, perhaps, the most oft-cited skill by the people I interviewed for the book. And for good reason. Communication is universal to virtually all industries and professions. Even the most isolated job types still include some kind of communication with the outside world, so learning to communicate clearly through a variety of mediums is crucial to your long-term success, regardless of what you do.

The thing about communication is that it is extremely diverse. Think about it. We communicate through both speaking and writing. Spoken communication also has many forms, from phone calls to formal presentations to difficult conversations with colleagues. The same goes for written communication, which has proliferated during the digital age. Texting, email and social media posts have exploded onto the scene, joining more traditional forms like letters, reports and memos.

Ambika talked about one of the most important yet overlooked aspects of good communication: developing a wide range of communication styles and being able to use them interchangeably depending on the context. For example, let's say you're the project manager that includes a wide variety of different stakeholders. When you're communicating with the engineering team, it's important to understand their preferred style, which tends to emphasize facts and data over emotions and narratives. But if you're communicating with the creative team, you might use a different strategy, employing metaphors and big ideas to get your points across. Ambika has found in her work with Zeit that this ability to shift communication styles for different environments, audiences and contexts is a universally transferable skill—and one that is highly sought after in many professional pathways.

So, what's the best way to develop your communication skills? The good news is that nearly everything in your life and your career requires communication, so there are plenty of opportunities to practice and improve. That being said, there are some very specific ways to develop your communication.

When it comes to speaking, one of the best ways to develop is to put yourself in challenging situations that require you to speak clearly to groups of people. Siya Sood, for example, cites her experience having to give verbal project updates and research reports to her seniors at the Albright Stonebridge Group as a kind of pressure cooker that taught her a whole lot about how to communicate. Being in challenging situations like that, allowed her to reach outside her comfort zone and get direct feedback from people with much more experience than her.

When it comes to writing, the opportunities to develop are all around us. Every text message and email gives us a chance to practice being a better communicator. The problem is that so many of us don't take writing seriously, unless we happen to be passionate about it. During school, many of us dread writing assignments and simply try to survive them. I think the most important step in becoming a better written communicator is cultivating a value for it. If you understand how important it is to communicate clearly, you'll naturally give more attention to it.

Remember, how you communicate will define to a significant degree how the world sees you. It's one of the primary ways you express yourself to everyone around you.

SIDEBAR: The Emotional Intelligence Revolution

One of the most often-cited 'soft skills' that people mention as important for modern careers is emotional intelligence. While the term was first coined in the 1960s, it gained global popularity in 1995 with the publication of science journalist Daniel Goleman's mega-bestselling book, *Emotional Intelligence: Why It Can Matter More Than IQ*. Simply put, emotional intelligence is the ability to identify and manage your own emotions and those of others you interact with. While I didn't identify emotional intelligence as one of the five general skill categories in this chapter, I consider it to be a driver of all of them, particularly in leadership and collaboration.

Inspired to a significant degree by Goleman's book, there has been a tremendous amount of research over the past two decades about the critical role that emotional intelligence plays in unlocking our professional capacities. In his seminal *Harvard Business Review* article, 'What Makes a Leader,' Goleman shares the results from competency research he's conducted among senior managers in nearly 200 companies around the world to show how emotional intelligence drives bottom line performance. For example, when comparing top-performing managers with their average-performing counterparts, 90 per cent of what set them apart fell within their emotional intelligence capabilities rather than their cognitive abilities.

How do you develop emotional intelligence? Goleman suggests that emotional intelligence is a skill that everyone can cultivate. To that end, he's broken it down into five subcomponents—self-awareness, self-regulation, motivation, empathy and social skills—each of which can be developed individually. The most important aspect of EI is self-awareness, which unlocks and amplifies all the others. As Laura Wilcox put it in a 2015 article for Harvard University's professional development blog, 'If you don't understand your own motivations and behaviours, it's nearly impossible to develop an understanding of others. A lack of self-awareness can also thwart your ability to think rationally and apply technical capabilities.'[5]

Collaboration

Perhaps the most important skill that Ambika cited is the ability to cultivate relationships with others. In fact, she's found, that strong relationship-builders tend to be far more successful in the long run than those who aren't. Why?

We live in a collaborative world and human beings are social creatures. As Ambika notes, nearly all jobs today are cross-functional and dynamic. We work in a wide variety of overlapping roles with different teams across multiple departments and projects. In this atmosphere, most projects are essentially being 'led from the side', as opposed to from the top. There's an inherent leadership role in everyone's job. That means that within any given project, you need to find ways to compel your teammates with your idea or your pitch, rather than through a more traditional, hierarchical and command structure. In order to thrive in this environment, you need to be able to build and maintain strong relationships with your teammates.

How do you do this? Ambika suggests that the key to strong relationship-building is being able to navigate a variety of backgrounds and work styles effectively. Many of us work in teams made up of people from different continents, age groups, educational backgrounds and political beliefs. Good collaborators are those who can take all those differences into account. People need to effectively read the room (real or virtual) and then temper their style and delivery appropriately. Cultivating this kind of relationship-building capacity takes immense practice and a considerable amount of attention towards those around you. That's why it's a rare and highly in-demand skill.

Another important aspect of relationship-building is the ability to deal with conflict. Anyone can get along with others when times are good and the pressure is low. But when tensions rise within your team or workplace, it's crucial that you embrace and deal with conflict constructively. The key to effective collaboration is the ability to understand and adeptly navigate the subtle dynamics that are inherent in all of the relationships and hierarchies of the workplace. Human relationships are messy. We aren't robots. We're full of all kinds of contradictions, paradoxes, good and bad qualities. Those who can understand this holistic picture of human nature and then translate that understanding to the complex world of relationships, can adeptly navigate even the most difficult and challenging workplace dynamics.

Critical Thinking

In the last chapter, I talked about Nikhil Sud and his passion for liberal arts education because it provides students with the ability to think critically. In fact, Nikhil believes that the number one capacity people should invest in is their ability to think. It's foundational to everything else we do and amplifies virtually every other important skill.

Nikhil is not alone. As we discussed in the last chapter, there is a growing concern among employers who find that the educational background is not giving young people the critical thinking skills they need to thrive in the workplace. Nikhil and many others attribute this to the rote-learning style that characterizes the standard Indian education system. Since students are generally not encouraged to ask questions or engage with what they're learning, they are essentially being trained to be 'learners not thinkers.' It encourages a kind of passivity in students that gets in the way of more active, critical thinking.

Thinking critically has many dimensions to it. It's a capacity to question what is presented to you and make up your own mind about its validity. It includes the ability to compare various concepts and identify patterns within them. It also includes the ability to sift through the overwhelming amounts of information that we are presented with on a daily basis and to separate fact from fiction so as to stitch together a cohesive perspective.

All these dimensions of critical thinking are becoming more and more important as the world around us speeds up. To thrive in this ever-shifting modern workplace, it's crucial that you invest in your own critical thinking capacities. There are countless ways to do this.

One of the best ways to improve your critical thinking, as we've discussed, is through your education. Attending a school with a rich academic culture is a good place to start, but regardless of where you go to school, you can make the extra effort to be an active participant in what you're learning. Don't just memorize concepts and facts, analyse them. Ask questions of your teachers and challenge yourself to understand the bigger picture within which any specific point exists. Don't just accept things at face value. Keep asking 'why' until you get to the core of an issue.

Another great way to develop and hone your critical thinking skills is to expose yourself to new ideas. This can take innumerable forms. Attending lectures or watching them online. Reading. Microsoft founder Bill Gates takes time each year to read a selection of books presenting new insights from a variety of disciplines. You can also build relationships with people you disagree with so you can challenge your own ideas to expand and learn to refine and fortify your own positions. When you expose yourself to new ideas, you're forced to think differently. And when you think differently, you have to compare your already-held positions in light of the new insights and opinions you're presented with. This comparison is the soil in which critical thinking grows.

One of the most effective practices for critical thinking is forming an opinion. Note that I didn't say 'having' an opinion. We all have plenty of opinions, most of which aren't well-formed. They've been given to us by family or society and we haven't thought them through. When you make the effort to form an opinion, your critical thinking kicks in. You have to do extensive research to consider multiple perspectives on an issue. You have to process plenty of information, much of which is conflicting, in order to distil and define your own predilection on any given subject.

Whatever approach you take, critical thinking is a lifelong pursuit—and one that will continue to pay long-term rewards.

Problem-Solving

The ability to solve problems is one of the most sought-after skills in the modern workplace, across all industries. Why? Problems are inevitable in nearly every job. The world is unpredictable and complex. Whether you're running a digital marketing campaign for a clothing brand or analysing X-rays in a medical facility, you're bound to run into problems in your work. Even the best-laid plans suffer setbacks. These can be technical, interpersonal, cultural or natural. Those who are able to effectively approach and solve problems, especially in a team environment, are highly in demand.

How Do You Become a Better Problem-Solver?

One of the lessons I learnt early on in my career is that I should not be surprised by the problems I encounter in any project. In fact, I shouldn't see them as problems at all, but as naturally occurring 'bumps' along the road of any project. And I've found this mentality to be at the core of good problem-solving. It seems simple, but it's a critical step. You don't want to be the person who is surprised when problems occur. It's better to be the one who expects them. Then you'll be prepared to work proactively towards a solution, rather than being frustrated, angry or shocked. You can get down to the business of attacking and solving the problem.

There are many reasons that I am grateful for my PhD in robotics. But perhaps more than anything else, that engineering background taught me how to solve problems. My career has gone in a very different direction from where it started out, traversing business consulting, education and entrepreneurship. But regardless of the context, any time I have faced a problem, I have approached its solution like an engineer: breaking it down into smaller components.

Most of the problems that require our attention are complex ones. They include different people, teams, technologies, timelines and moving parts. So, the first step I always take when I approach a problem is to break it down into the smallest possible parts. This helps to reduce a seemingly overwhelming problem into a much more manageable exercise. It also forces you to define the problem you're actually trying to solve, which can often be totally at variance with what you originally thought.

Let's use an example from recent history to illustrate this point. In 2002, Elon Musk decided that he wanted to put a greenhouse on Mars, which he saw as a critical step in eventually being able to populate the planet. To get the greenhouse to Mars, Musk needed a rocket and the going rate for a Mars-bound rocket in those days was more than his $20 billion budget for the project. He decided to take matters into his own hands. He began to 'break down' the construction of a rocket into its component pieces and realized that if he could build and construct the various parts himself, he could dramatically reduce his costs. In fact, he found that the raw materials required to build the rockets represented only 3 per cent of the sales price. To that end, he founded the SpaceX programme and developed the Falcon 1 rocket, which in 2008 became the first privately funded rocket to orbit the earth. While he's yet to get his greenhouse to Mars, he has solved a critical problem in the long-term mission to inhabit distant planets: affordable rockets.

In my interview with Anita Mackenzie, she pointed out another important element of the problem-solving skill that I'd yet to seriously consider: the DIY movement. As she learned when she left the corporate world to start her own design company, Plum Chutney, there are tremendous opportunities to quickly acquire the new skills necessary to solve a wide variety of problems. The internet has, in a way, empowered all of us to become 'mini-experts' in a wide range of subjects and therefore solve a lot of problems that in the past we would have had to depend on others for. Using everything from online courses, to YouTube videos, to collaborations with freelancers, to online companies that solve niche problems, the resources available to those who want to 'do it themselves' are greater than ever.

When Anita decided to create a retail design business, she had to solve a lot of problems herself: website design, e-commerce, digital marketing, commercial real estate, product-sourcing, etc. She remarked how her corporate training hadn't prepared her for this new reality, because so many of these functions were provided for her. As a solopreneur, she had to learn how to quickly teach herself new skills and solve the endless stream of new 'problems' she encountered in trying to set up and run her company.

Whether you're a solopreneur or working for a large company, learning to be a 'self-solver' is a critical skill for you to develop. It will empower you to be more independent and make you more attractive for employers who need proactive employees with the ability to approach the inevitable problems they face with poise, clarity and ingenuity.

Leadership

During her tenure at McKinsey India, Siya Sood learned a lesson about leadership that she credits as being a turning point in her career. She was part of a small team that was assigned with organizing a company retreat that would include directors from around the country. Two weeks before the event, her direct manager quit and she was thrown into the position of being the lead organizer of the retreat; she had only one other teammate to help her make it a success. She was young—only a few years out of graduate school—so the challenge before her was immense. But she embraced it, stepping up in a way that she had never done in her life up to that point.

The event ended up being a huge success and Siya received a lot of praise from the senior director for her efforts to rise up and take charge in a difficult situation. The experience gave her a big shot of well-earned confidence and taught her a valuable lesson about leadership that has fuelled her ever since: if you're willing to take responsibility and hold yourself and those around you to a high standard of excellence, you will find yourself indispensable to any team, project or company you're a part of.

Not surprisingly, leadership is a skill that most organizations desperately need. This 'leadership gap', as it has come to be known, has been talked about and focused on for well over a decade now, yet it still persists. In a 2015 survey of global organizations, for example, the World Economic Forum found that 86 per cent of respondents felt that there is still a global leadership crisis.[6] The great irony of the leadership gap is that the level of talent and sheer cognitive power within organizations has never been higher. Companies have done a commendable job of finding and cultivating their intellectual capital. And yet, in spite of all that, study after study and book after book find the same thing: there's a lack of strong leadership in virtually every industry.

Why? Leadership may be the most difficult skill to cultivate, because it can only really be taught through experience. There is a whole industry dedicated to training leaders and much of what is being taught is quite useful. But in order for any of these lessons or principles to really take hold within any aspiring leader, there must be an orientation of fundamental responsibility like the one Siya discovered for herself. You can have all the leadership training in the world, but if you're unwilling to challenge yourself by taking responsibility for whatever team or project you're a part of, none of it will end up becoming relevant.

So, if leadership training won't necessarily teach you how to lead, what should you do to cultivate this skill? Again, I'm not discounting the value of leadership training and I advise everyone to pursue it in some form. But in order for any leadership tools to become relevant to your own life or career, you need to find opportunities to test yourself. Get experience. Take risks. Sign up to take on projects or positions that feel a little uncomfortable and just beyond reach. For Siya, she was only able to tap into her innate leadership abilities by stepping up to a challenge. And in my experience, that's really the only way it works.

Exercises

Below are a series of questions and exercises you can use to start to think about your own skill set and how you might update it to help you in your life and career. Feel free to approach them in whichever order makes the most sense for you and skip any that you don't find relevant:

1. Think of your own professional goals. Do you have the skills to achieve them?
2. Do a self-assessment of your skills based on the five general categories in this chapter. Would you say you are below average, average or above average in each skill?
3. Ask a trusted friend, colleague, or mentor to rate you on these five skills. How do their answers compare with yours?
4. Review your answers to the first two questions. For the skills where you are average or below, brainstorm some things you can do to improve upon them. For

the skills where you are above average, brainstorm some ways that you can leverage those capacities to improve in your current job, academic pathway and/ or your future career.

5. Interview someone who you admire about the skills they've found most useful in their own career. Be sure to ask for advice about how to cultivate those skills.

5

Picking Up (and Connecting) the Dots

In his famous 2005 commencement address at Stanford University, the late Apple founder Steve Jobs gave a compelling piece of wisdom that has inspired a generation of young people to move forward courageously into an unknown and uncertain future. Reflecting on the diverse experiences that shaped his own life and career, he said, 'You can't connect the dots looking forward; you can only connect them looking backward. So, you have to trust that the dots will somehow connect in your future.'

Jobs' words, like so much of his life's work, have turned out to be quite prescient. With each passing decade, the world is becoming less and less predictable and it's becoming more and more difficult to connect the dots of our lives and careers looking forward. There's just too much of an element of the unknown. The world ten years from now will likely be dramatically different than it is today, and so all of us have a tremendous challenge before us, as we prepare for that unpredictable future. His metaphor speaks to the courage it takes to chart a career without knowing exactly where you're going, which is becoming an essential ingredient for anyone who wants to navigate the world we're living in successfully.

And while I am deeply inspired by Jobs' advice, there is one complementary piece I'd like to add to it. If you want to be able to *connect* the dots in your own life, you have to be willing to *pick them up* first. For Jobs, picking up the dots meant being willing to test out a variety of experiences that would eventually converge into his life's work: Apple computers and all its revolutionary products. He cites one such dot as enrolling in a college calligraphy class for no other reason than the fact that he was curious about it. And then, ten years later, drawing upon that experience to develop the first computer ever created with beautiful typography. The point is that had he never been willing to take a risk and 'pick up that dot', he would never have been able to connect it to the seemingly unrelated process of computer engineering.

The willingness to pick up new experiences was a universal quality among everyone I interviewed. None of their career paths were linear. All were interspersed with twists and turns. But all of them found a way to alchemize their diverse experiences and skills into something uniquely fulfilling and impactful. Driving each of them was a willingness to experiment, take risks and continually try new experiences.

In this chapter we're going to explore this process of picking up and eventually connecting the dots through the stories of some of our interviewees. We'll talk about the importance of being willing to take risks and experiment with your life and career. We'll discuss the natural fear of failure that most of us seem to have and how to transcend it. We'll talk about the value of the real-world experience and how to get it even when you're just starting out. Finally, we'll explore how to stitch everything together in your own career.

Your Life Is an Experiment

Paroma Roy Chowdhury is a self-described 'shapeshifter'—a label that perfectly sums up her squiggly career. When Paroma received a graduate degree in international relations back in the early 1990s, she could never have envisioned where her professional journey would take her: from covering business news for some of India's largest newspapers to running career services for a premier business school to serving as corporate communications executive for some of the biggest companies in the world, including GE, SoftBank, Google and her current position with India's largest EdTech company, BYJU'S.

Over that time, she has pivoted career tracks and jumped between industries, often having no formal experience in the field she was entering. To many people, this unprecedented leap of faith would have been terrifying. To Paroma, they were challenges to be embraced. Paroma's life philosophy revolves around having the courage to take risks and approach her own career as one grand experiment. With each experiment she has picked up dots that eventually lead to the next phase of her career.

Paroma's first experiment came after graduate school. Rather than continuing the normal pathway by moving into a PhD programme, she decided to pursue her passion for journalism, cultivated by working for various school newspapers. She took a job with the *Business Standard* working on the business desk, even though she had no business experience. Paroma had never read a business paper nor done a balance sheet, but she didn't let that stop or deter her. She dug in and used the job as a training opportunity—one that prepared her to eventually take a job as business editor for the *Economic Times*, which was the largest business daily in Asia at the time and then *Business Today*, one of India's widest-read English-language magazines.

By 2001, Paroma had spent a decade in business journalism and was ready for her next experiment; she just didn't quite know it yet. After completing a journalism fellowship at Cambridge University, Paroma was scouted by the fledgling Indian School of Business, which is where our paths first crossed. We had become aware of her reputation in the business world and thought that her skill set and connections would be an asset to us as we attempted to grow ISB's reach within India's booming business world. Even though she had an established career and family life in Delhi, we convinced her to come on board with ISB, working in Hyderabad during the week and flying home on the weekends.

Paroma describes that pivot as 'crazy' due to the awkward logistics and her lack of experience. But like everything else in her life, she took the leap and it ended up being enormously rewarding. She ran our career services department and was tasked with selling our programmes to corporations. It was a difficult job, because ISB was still considered an imposter by many in the business world at the time, but she persevered and ended up being an instrumental piece in the growth of the school during that period.

It was through her experience at ISB that Paroma picked up a dot that would launch the next experiment of her career. ISB hosted a lecture series and Paroma had the privilege of hosting one of the guest speakers; Tyger Tyagarajan, who worked for General Electric's Capital International Services (GECIS), which would eventually become GenPact. They struck a friendship and he was so impressed with her that he told his boss, Pramod Bhasin, to hire her even though he wasn't sure for what position.

Paroma was shocked when she got the call from GE offering her a job running communications and executive branding for GE Capital. She was intrigued by the opportunity and flew to Bangalore for a particularly intense interview with Bhasin, who was known to be quite tough. During their conversation, Bhasin asked her, 'Do you have any experience with corporate communications?' Her answer was, 'No, but I can write.' And the rest is history. As with each of Paroma's many career pivots, she didn't let a lack of formal experience stop her from breaking into a new field. She got the job with GE and began a long and illustrious career in corporate communications.

While Paroma has remained in the field of corporate communications for the last two decades, she hasn't stopped experimenting. She's continued to jump into new industries, taking positions at Hewlett Packard, AirTel, SoftBank and Google. With each leap, she entered an industry with which she had little if any familiarity and has picked up many new dots as a result. In her latest job with the EdTech company, BYJU'S, she loves the challenge of running communications in a field that is completely foreign to her.

There are many lessons to be learned from Paroma's successful non-linear career, but perhaps most important is the willingness to take risks and try new things. Her advice to young people is to be willing to experiment with your career. Follow your instincts and always try new things. If they don't work out, you can also shift into something else. Your career, in this way, can be a kind of experiment. Every new opportunity is a hypothesis from which you gather new data. You can then use it to build your next hypothesis and continue the process of experimenting, learning and growing forever.

Overcoming the Fear of Failure

Uday Shankar is a giant in the world of Indian media and entertainment. Like so many people in the book, his pathway has been a winding one, full of pivots that ultimately led him to where he is today. Till recently, he was the CEO of Disney Asia Pacific, he started as a newspaperman for the *Times of India* before shifting into broadcast journalism with Zee TV, then becoming CEO of Star Entertainment and finally setting up Bodhi Tree Systems, a multi-billion dollar platform that has already invested in education and media. His impressive career trajectory has been fuelled by a passion to use different forms of media to drive social change and what he calls 'a scant regard for failure'.

When I asked Uday to share his best advice for young people who are at the very beginning of their career, his answer was fast and simple: don't be afraid to fail. 'The fear of failure,' he says, 'is the main thing that holds people back from achieving their goals.'

For Uday, this isn't just advice. It's a principle he's lived by his whole career and one that guided him through what may have been the biggest and most difficult decisions of his career. Uday attended Jawaharlal Nehru University and, after graduating with an MPhil degree, took a job with the *Times of India*, covering rural issues across the country. He thoroughly enjoyed the job, but in the early '90s, encountered something that would change his life forever: television. It was CNN coverage of the first Gulf War, broadcast on a little TV attached to a large satellite dish with a group of people huddled around to watch in amazement. In that moment, Uday realized that this form of media, which was relatively new in India at the time, had the potential to influence hearts and minds far more than the written word ever could. So, he became engrossed and obsessed.

The problem was that there were very few opportunities to work in TV in India at that time. Uday's only option was a low-level position that paid less than half of what he was making at the time. Everyone, including his wife, thought he was crazy. He had a great newspaper career— one that he had worked hard to build. How could he support his family on such a low salary? And why would he waste all the time he'd invested in his current field to essentially start over in this new and unproven industry?

Again, Uday was not afraid to fail, so he took the job. The gamble eventually paid off. He worked his way up through the ranks in the fledgling broadcasting industry and launched what would end up being one of the most successful careers in the Indian media history.

While overcoming the fear of failure won't necessarily lead you to the kind of success that Uday has enjoyed in his career, it is a crucial ingredient if you want to be able to take advantage of the opportunities that will inevitably come your way. If you're going to be able to pick up those dots, you're likely to encounter at least some of this fear in yourself—and learn to deal with it.

Fear of failure has long been known as one of the biggest psychological obstacles to success. According to a 2018 study by Norwest Venture Partners, 90 per cent of the CEOs they interviewed 'admit fear of failure keeps them up at night more than any other concern.'[1] In response to this risk-averse human tendency, 'fail fast,' has become a kind of mantra in the tech world among innovators who are working to stay ahead of the curve. And there have been many self-help books written on the subject. There's even a psychological term for the fear of failure: atychiphobia.

But while Uday is not the first to tout overcoming atychiphobia as a crucial element of any successful career, he offers an interesting twist that I've yet to encounter. He suggests that while it's crucial that you overcome your fear of failure in order to try new things, once you commit to a path, you should do everything you can not to fail. I find this to be a helpful guardrail against the kind of recklessness that can often accompany this high-risk mentality. In other words, overcoming your fear of failure helps you to seize opportunities and take action; but once you've made your decision, you need to do everything in your power not to fail.

So, what's the best way to overcome your fear of failure? Uday's main advice is to not take yourself too seriously. Psychologists have suggested that a big component of fearing failure is actually a fear of being *seen* as a failure. So, one of the best ways to help you overcome your fear of failure is to stop taking yourself so seriously. If 'you' are not that big of a deal, then it doesn't matter if 'you' are seen as a failure or a success. This can help release the psychological burden that's perpetually holding you back from taking risks.

Another useful way to overcome your fear of failure is to reframe what 'failure' means. Earlier in this chapter we talked about Paroma's willingness to see her life as an experiment. In an experiment, there are no right or wrong results; there's only more data you can use to create your next experiment. So, from this vantage point, a 'failed' venture or job or choice, isn't a failure at all. It's an opportunity to learn, grow and refine.

Finally, perhaps the best way to overcome your fear of failure is to actually fail. Try new things and take some risks that don't pan out. You'll quickly find out that failure is not so bad. You'll find that you recover from failure faster than you would have expected. You'll go on living and growing. The more you fail, the more you'll realize how benign it actually is.

SIDEBAR: Intelligent Failure

Most people have probably heard of the term 'fail fast.' It has become popular in the start-up business world to encourage companies to take big, bold risks that often fail in order to gather data that can be used to create the next iteration of a product or system. It's also seeped into the world of personal development as a kind of antidote to the fear of failure, helping people to take more risks and grow.

While I agree with the concept of failing fast to a degree, it can also be dangerous if taken too far. Failure can actually have big consequences in your life if you're not careful. For this reason, I prefer the term 'intelligent failure', which was first coined by Duke University's Sim Sitkin in his 1996 article, 'Learning through failure: The strategy of small losses' for the *Journal of Organizational Learning*.[2]

As the title of his article suggests, Sitkin's idea of intelligent failure was based on gathering insights from a series of smaller failures. In his view, these smaller failures are the result of a very clearly thought through initiative. In other words, you're not throwing caution to the wind and recklessly attempting to do big things. Rather, you're taking on challenges or initiatives that you have considered and prepared for, but that you understand might not work perfectly. You're ready for failure. More importantly, you're ready to learn from that failure.

How do you learn to fail intelligently? Here are a few general guidelines:

- In order to be able to fail intelligently, it's best to be in environments where experimentation is encouraged and failure is accepted. You can help create these environments in your own life or seek them out.
- Challenge yourself by taking on difficult tasks where you will likely experience some degree of failure. In doing this, you'll become more comfortable from failure and learn how to learn from it.
- Adjust your mindset to see failure as a natural part of a creative life. This will help you to become more comfortable with and tolerant of failure in yourself and others.
- Make sure that you are not trying to fail. Rather, you're doing your best not to fail, but ready to learn from any failure that might occur.

You Don't Have to Feel Like an Imposter

Smridhi Marwah has never been one to back down from a challenge. After graduating top of her class in a Masters in Public Health programme, she chose to go into the non-profit world, rather than taking a more secure and high-paying job in the government. She had a passion to help make the world a better place and wanted to prove that she could build a successful career out of doing it. After a short stint with an animal rights group (the Federation of Indian Animal Protection Organizations), she got a job working for a global non-profit called Live to Love, which runs a wide variety of projects to help serve and empower the indigenous people of the Himalayan region. And she has thrived in that role.

Originally hired in communications, she quickly exhibited a penchant for fundraising and was soon offered a position as the Director of Development, a job that she had no formal training for. The Live to Love organization has significant partners around the world. As part of her role as the Director of Development, Smridhi, who was still quite young for such a position, found herself in meetings and at events with many high-level and often intimidating people.

In these instances, Smridhi came face to face with a feeling that many young people encounter in their careers: a sense that she didn't deserve to be there—because of her age, or lack of intelligence or whatever negative self-belief was going through her head. Some call this 'imposter syndrome'. Also known as 'perceived fraudulence', it's essentially the psychological experience of being unable to accept one's own success, attributing any accomplishments you've achieved to luck, rather than hard work or talent. It often comes with a kind of all-pervasive fear that you will eventually be 'found out' or discovered to be a fraud in whatever situation you're in.

This was particularly strong for Smridhi, given how quickly she moved into such an important role in her organization. But she didn't let the feeling of imposter syndrome hold her back. By learning to identify it in herself, she was able to see through it and find the confidence to perform well in high-pressure environments. She proved to herself, over and over again, that she didn't have to feel like an imposter in any new situation she found herself in, no matter how unqualified she might have perceived herself to be.

It turns out that imposter syndrome is actually quite pervasive. The condition was first identified by a team of psychologists, Suzanne Imes, PhD, and Pauline Rose Clance, PhD, in 1978 who originally attributed it primarily to women. Since that time, of course, imposter syndrome has been shown to have no gender preference and is something that most of us encounter. A 2011 article in the *Journal of Behavioral Science*, for example, found that 70 per cent of people surveyed report that they have experienced some form of imposter syndrome at some point in their lives.[3]

While the majority of people have some experience of imposter syndrome, there has been substantial research showing that it is particularly strong for high-achieving individuals. But it isn't just personality types that drive this condition. There's also an important cultural component. In a landmark paper on the subject published in the *Frontiers in Psychology Journal*, research found that 'external' forces help to create an environment where feelings of 'perceived fraudulence' are more common. These forces often take the form of a high pressure to succeed from family, school or even society as a whole.[4]

So, what can you do to deal with imposter syndrome in yourself? The first step is to become aware of it as a condition, as Smridhi did. When you feel inadequate or like you're a fraud, it's probably a good sign as you're experiencing some version of imposter syndrome. Just knowing that can help you to take a step back and question your conclusions. You can look at the facts of a situation and see that you probably have earned your success and do deserve to be in the situation you're in.

One of the best ways to gain objectivity on your experience is to talk to someone else. You can approach a friend, colleague or mentor and share what you're going through. Since imposter syndrome is a subjective distortion of reality, by getting input from someone outside of your own head, you can help to see yourself more objectively. A vulnerable conversation about your assumptions can quickly show and prove them to be false.

Lastly, it's important to remember that you probably can't cure yourself of imposter syndrome. If you're an ambitious, high-achieving person who throws yourself into challenging opportunities, you will probably always experience these feelings of inadequacy to some degree. So, you shouldn't expect them to go away. Instead, be ready for them, understand them and find a way to work through them.

Get as Much Experience as You Can

I've heard some version of the following story from various young people who are trying to break into the job market. They interview for a job and their potential employer is impressed by them, but doesn't offer them a job because they don't have enough professional experience. And they inevitably say something like, 'But how can I get professional experience if no one will hire me due to a lack of experience?'

This experience conundrum points to a crucial insight about modern careers. Experience is everything. You can have all the education in the world, but it can't replace real-world experience. Your tangible work experience will make up the majority of the dots that you pick up and connect along the way. As we discussed in Chapter 2 in our exploration about self-discovery, most of us don't know much about ourselves—what we want to do with our lives and what we are good at—until we get concrete working experience.

So how do you get real-world experience, especially when you're starting out? One avenue is through the growing number of experiential learning programmes that are available through colleges and universities. Programmes like the Young India Fellowship at Ashoka University and others like it, are designed to expose students to a wide range of subjects and professionals as part of their undergraduate or graduate studies. Additionally, many offer experiential learning where they are working with real-world case studies and current events as part of their educational process.

As you may recall from Chapter 2, I met Monica Hariharan at YIF and it was through her participation in the programme where she was able to gain direct experience of the possibilities available to her in the working world. Monica came to YIF with a passionate, but narrowly defined desire to find a career that would make a social difference in the world. She had originally pursued journalism as an avenue to make a positive social impact, but that wasn't satisfying. Before enrolling in YIF, she had even considered joining the Indian Army and had begun all the physical training to prepare herself. But when she enrolled at YIF, she was exposed to an eclectic mix of academics and professionals who were working, in their own unique ways, to make a social difference. They didn't fit her original, stereotypical definition of activists, but soon she saw through that limited perception and opened herself up to a wide range of career possibilities that she would have never even considered before.

Another way to get direct experience is by volunteering for extra assignments within your current job or school. Take Siya Sood, for example. In the last chapter, we talked about how her experience organizing a company retreat taught her a valuable lesson and gained the attention of her superiors. This was an assignment that Siya had asked for, not something assigned to her. She was proactively seeking more experiences within the role she already had that would help her grow, network and develop new skills. Regardless of what your position is within your organization or school, you usually have the opportunity to seek out new opportunities for growth. You can volunteer to take on extra responsibilities or even suggest new initiatives that you think would be of value. The key is to find creative ways to gain more experience and in doing so, pick up more dots that will eventually connect to the squiggly threads of your career.

SIDEBAR: Curiosity Is a Superpower

According to Uday Shankar, curiosity is the most underrated skill in the world. It's a quality that he credits with helping him sustain a high level of success throughout his career. 'I'm curious about everything,' he told me. 'If I'm eating a good meal, I'm curious about how it was made. If I hear about a new idea, I want to learn everything I can about it. Curiosity has helped me to continuously grow throughout my career.'

Unfortunately, curiosity tends to be a fairly rare quality, especially among adults. When we are children, we are curious about everything we encounter, but as we grow up, that curiosity tends to dissipate. In a 2011 TEDx Talk entitled 'The Failure of Success,' Dr George Land shares the results of a study he conducted to measure the decreasing levels of curiosity over time. Administering a series of 'curiosity tests' he had developed at NASA to 1600 children over the course of a decade, he found that curiosity levels dramatically decreased over time from 98 per cent curiosity scores on average at age five to only 12 per cent at age fifteen. When he later gave the test to adults, the number dropped to 2 per cent.[5]

Why the drop in curiosity as we get older? In a 2008 study published in *Psychological Science,* researchers found that our decrease in curiosity over time is likely due to the fact that as we age, we accumulate more knowledge.[6] In other words, the more we know (or think we know), the less curious we become about what we don't already know.

But while there might be a natural decrease in our curiosity over time, it doesn't mean we can't actively cultivate it, much like Uday has throughout his career. And there are many arguments for doing so. In her 2018 article for the *Harvard Business Review*, 'The Business Case for Curiosity', behavioural scientist Francesca Gino cites a wide variety of studies to highlight the impact of curiosity on workplace performance. One major benefit is that curiosity can protect us from confirmation bias, which helps us to make more accurate assessments of situations and take better decisions. Gino also cites a study conducted by INSEAD researcher Spencer Harrison at a call centre, which found that employees with higher levels of curiosity exercised more workplace creativity and productivity.[7]

How do you increase your curiosity? While there are many strategies and exercises, the consensus around the best way to book your curiosity is by asking more questions. Don't just accept the world at face value, ask why things are the way they are. It's a simple exercise, but it will tap into your innate curiosity and open your mind up to what you don't already know.

Putting It All Together

As the great Steve Jobs said in the commencement address that I referred to at the beginning of this chapter: you can only connect the dots of your life looking backward. And as I added to his insight, in order to connect these dots in the future, you need to pick them up in the present. As we come to the end of this chapter, I want to leave you with one final story about the dots I picked up in my own career.

When I started out as an engineering student at the Indian Institute of Technology in the 1980s, I could never have imagined that one day I would end up as the founding Dean of what has grown to become India's most renowned business school. Nor could I have foreseen becoming an entrepreneur or a business consultant. I was just a young man following the pathways before me.

But along the way, like Uday and Paroma, I was presented with many opportunities to take risks and try new things. Some of them worked and others didn't. But each presented me with a chance to learn and to grow. They became part of me and my legacy. They became dots that I eventually connected to create the web that is my own squiggly career. If I hadn't picked up these dots, I would have never been able to connect them.

As you're reading this, you might see this call to action as intimidating. It might feel uncomfortable to take the risks before you and confront your fear of failure. But there's also something very liberating about this position. You don't have to figure it all out before you get on with the next steps in your career. You don't have to feel the unnecessary pressure to get it right. You can try things, experiment and feel free to make mistakes. That's the thing about modern careers. Change is a constant. They're messy and squiggly and don't necessarily follow a predictable pattern. If you can find freedom in this chaos, you will thrive.

Exercises

Below you'll find some exercises and reflections you can use to help you connect your own 'dots' and explore your relationship to risk and the fear of failure. Feel free to skip around and engage them in any order you prefer, or skip them altogether.

1. Reflect on your own life and think of the important 'dots' that you have picked up thus far. These could

be experiences or achievements. There are no right or wrong answers.

2. If you draw a figurative line between these dots, is it straight or squiggly? Do you see any patterns emerging? Are there any connections that surprise you?

3. What are the biggest risks you've taken in your life? How did you feel before taking the risk? What made you go for it? How did you feel after making the leap? What did you learn from the experience?

4. Are there any risks that you were compelled by but ended up not taking in the end? Why did you decide to pass on the opportunity? Do you regret your decision?

5. Consider your current work or educational situation. You might have a job or be a student. What opportunities do you have available to you to gain more real-world experiences?

6

The Power of Mentorship

Back in the late 1990s, I was faced with one of the most difficult decisions of my career. I was working as a consultant at McKinsey and Company and one of my many projects in that role was to help set up the Indian School of Business (ISB) in Hyderabad. While setting up educational institutions was not core to McKinsey, Rajat Kumar Gupta, the then Global Managing Director, saw the value in establishing a world-class business school in India to help train a new generation of managers to meet the growing demands of India's burgeoning economy.

The project took years of planning and included collaborations with business leaders from both the US and India, as well as several international business schools, including the Wharton School at the University of Pennsylvania and the Kellogg School of Management at Northwestern University. As we neared the launch of the school, the two esteemed academics we had tapped to serve as the founding Deans dropped out, which put us in quite a conundrum. The ISB Board's solution was to ask me to step in and take on the position.

I was shocked by the offer. I was only thirty-seven years old at the time and had virtually no experience in academia, outside of my own education and less than two years post-PhD. I had worked on the ISB launch more as a passion project at McKinsey and it was far from my primary professional focus. How could I possibly be qualified for a position like this? What about my career with McKinsey? Yet there was also something very compelling about the opportunity. I had an instinct that this was something that I would like to do and I was excited by the challenge it presented.

But I was facing tremendous resistance. In order to take the position of dean, I would need to take a leave of absence from McKinsey. My colleagues were, understandably, against the move. I was a partner at the time and was a key point of contact with many of our biggest clients. My fellow partners were worried that my absence would have a negative impact on some of our most important corporate relationships.

There was also the issue of my career. I was warned by many trusted colleagues and friends that stepping away from McKinsey, even for a short time, could jeopardize my future advancement within the firm. I was on a senior partner track, after all and the move to ISB could damage my standing within McKinsey and potentially waste the time and effort I had put in to get to where I was in my career to that point. Even my own wife was against the ISB move and felt that it was too big a risk for me to take. At the time, I honestly didn't have the courage to stand up to the many people in my life who advised me not to take the job. And I nearly didn't take it.

But that's when I had a conversation with Don Jacobs, a trusted mentor, that would potentially change my life forever. Jacobs was the Dean of Kellogg and served as a founding board member of ISB. When I asked him what I should do, he was unequivocal. 'Take the job,' he advised, 'This is a no-brainer.'

I voiced the concerns over what it would do for my career at McKinsey, to which he said something along the lines of, 'Are you kidding me? Sure, your career might suffer, marginally. But think of what you'll be gaining in return. You have the opportunity to build an institution that will outlast you; and it's being served to you on a platter. This will be your legacy. You will always be known as the Founding Dean of what will likely be one of India's premier business schools.'

It turns out that Don was right. I took the job as Founding Dean of ISB and while I did eventually go back to McKinsey, the move sparked a long and fascinating career in the world of education, something I never would have anticipated in my younger years. I have since been involved in starting several more academic institutions and in a way, education has become my life's work.

Had it not been for that conversation with Don all those years ago, I would probably not have taken the ISB job and experienced everything that happened as a result. That's the power of mentorship. Mentors can help you see the dots in your own life—the connections between them—that you're simply unable to see yourself. They can step in during critical moments to give you the clarity and confidence you need to make a big move with your life. They can act as guardrails for your own career, keeping you on track when you need it and urging you to break out of your existing box when the timing is right.

Mentorship, it turns out, is one of the most important ingredients in a successful career. Nearly everyone I interviewed for the book said that mentors played a key role in their early professional and educational decisions and also helped them through many of the critical junctures of their journey. Mentors helped them to identify their strengths, refine their passions and push them towards higher degrees of excellence. They held them to a higher standard of excellence than they could themselves. They served as examples they could model their own careers after. And they gave them the confidence and perspective to make big pivots when the time was right.

In many ways, mentorship can help amplify all of the other elements of the book thus far: discovering your passions, strengths and weaknesses; choosing the right educational path; assessing and cultivating the right skill sets and helping you connect the dots of your own career. In this chapter we'll draw upon the experience of the interviewees to explore the importance of mentorship and offer practical advice about the best ways to find and engage a mentor.

SIDEBAR: Mentorship Works

I have come across countless stories about the positive role that mentors play in people's careers. This includes my own career, of course, as well as many of the people

I interviewed for this book. But the evidence for the power of mentorship isn't just anecdotal. There has been a plethora of research conducted to measure the tangible benefits of mentorship on everything from performance to job satisfaction to employee retention.

Sun Microsystems partnered with Gartner Research and Capital Analytics to conduct a study of 1000 employees over a five-year period to measure the impact of mentorship on their company. They found that 25 per cent of employees who participated in the mentoring programme had a salary increase, compared to only 5 per cent of those who didn't. Additionally, mentees were promoted five times more often than employees with no mentors.[1] According to the 2020 Vistage CEO Confidence Survey Index, of the 1300 CEOs surveyed, 86 per cent said that mentors have been critical to their professional success.[2]

Mentorship also has an impact on job satisfaction. A 2019 Workplace Happiness Survey conducted by CNBC and SurveyMonkey, which surveyed 8000 employees across many industries, found that 91 per cent of workers with mentors are 'satisfied' with their jobs, while 57 per cent say they are 'very satisfied.' Both of these numbers dropped by at least ten percentage points among employees without mentors. The same survey found that over 40 per cent of workers without mentors have considered quitting their job, compared to only 25 per cent for those who have mentors.[3]

The positive impact of mentorship isn't just limited to the working world. Students also benefit from having mentors. A 2020 study published in the *Journal of Advanced Medical Education and Professionalism* tracked the impacts of a mentorship programme on 148 students at the Al Azhar Medical College in Kerala. They found that the mean exam scores among students increased significantly after participating in the mentorship programme; and this impact was particularly high among the below average students.[4]

A Trusted Voice Outside of Your Family

Srikant Sastri has made a second career out of mentorship. After retiring from a decade long stint of starting, growing and eventually selling two different companies, Srikant wanted to give back by mentoring aspiring entrepreneurs who were looking for guidance as they attempted to get their own ventures off the ground. To that end, he began teaching entrepreneurship at universities, in start-up incubators and through his own workshops. He jokes that because of his penchant for working with young entrepreneurs, he spends more time with people his sons' age than with people of his own generation like me (Srikant and I attended school together at the Indian Institute of Technology Kanpur).

While Srikant has a lot to say about the benefits of mentorship, from his experience as both a mentor and a mentee, he brought up a unique point about the role mentors can play in Indian society that I haven't heard anywhere else. A mentor, especially a reputable one, can be a source of objective advice from outside the family that can help provide legitimacy to decisions that might seem outside the comfort zone of your parents or relatives.

This is particularly important in Indian culture, where parents tend to be more active in the lives of their children even after college and in the early years of their career. As Srikant points out, having a mentor can help give your family trust that you are getting good advice, even if it doesn't necessarily line up with their own.

In her *New York Times* bestselling memoir, *My Life In Full: Work, Family, and Our Future* (Penguin, 2021), Indian-American executive Indra Nooyi tells a story about her own experience with mentorship that underscores Srikant's point. Nooyi, who served as the CEO of PepsiCo for over a decade and was ranked by *Forbes* magazine as the second most powerful businesswomen in 2017, got her start in business working for the textile company Mettur Beardsell in Madras. With Nooyi leaving the company for a position at Johnson & Johnson after a worker strike, Mettur Beardsell offered her a senior management position if she would come back and work for them. At the same time, she had applied and been accepted to the Yale School of Management and was very excited about the opportunity the programme offered her to grow in her career and break into the US business world.

As she tells it, Nooyi was conflicted. Taking the job at Mettur Beardsell would make her one of the youngest women to have such a senior position in the Indian business world. There was a lot of money and prestige associated with the position and a strong argument for taking the offer. But she felt more compelled by the Yale offer. She didn't know what to do, so she turned to one of her mentors Norman Wade for advice. Wade, admittedly, was not the most objective advisor since he was a director at Mettur Beardshell. But as Nooyi tells it, Wade gave her advice as he would to his daughter, not as a business executive and told her to go to Yale.

When Nooyi told her parents that she wanted to turn down the Mettur Beardshell offer and go to Yale, their first question was, 'What does Norman think?' When she shared Wade's endorsement of Yale with their family, they trusted the decision and gave her their blessings to go.

Of course, your family won't always blindly trust what your mentor says or consider their advice to be the gospel truth, but they can be a crucial advocate for your future. And this isn't just to help you 'sell' what you want to do to your family. A mentor is someone who can often be more objective about you than your family can. A good mentor's primary interest should be your own personal future, without having their own agenda in the way that family members often can. They will also be able to see you more objectively than your family can. In this way, a mentor will be more focused on who you will be in the future than who you have been in the past.

Helping You to Find and Connect the Dots

In Chapter 2, we explored the importance of self-discovery—of understanding what your hidden talents are, of figuring out what you're passionate about, of deciding what you want to do with your career. One of the key points I made about self-discovery is that it's something that happens gradually throughout your career. Most of us aren't completely clear about what we want to do with our lives from a very young age. We need to experiment and gain experience to start to learn about who we are.

Mentors can play a huge role in this organic process of self-discovery. They can be an objective observer of our career and help us to see the 'dots' that we've already picked up or have a chance to pick up and advise us on how to integrate them into the web of our careers. They can point to talents or experiences that we might otherwise overlook and show us how to leverage them into new opportunities and experiences.

I have experienced this from both sides of the mentorship coin, as a mentor and a mentee. I've been fortunate to have extraordinary mentors of my own, as I discussed at the beginning of this chapter. And through my work in education, I've been lucky enough to come into contact with many bright young people and play the role of a mentor for some of them. One of my most memorable experiences of mentorship was with Siya Sood, whom we met in Chapter 2 of this book.

At the end of Siya's participation in the Vedica Scholars Programme for Women, she and many of her peers began to receive job placement offers. One of Siya's discoveries during the eighteen-month postgraduate programme was that she had a knack for communications. It was not only something she was interested in, but also something she was good at. So, when she received an offer for a Public Relations position, she was convinced that she should take it. She brought the offer to her two advisors, myself and my colleague and now Harappa co-founder Shreyasi Singh and we immediately saw what she couldn't see. While the job was, indeed, relevant to her skills and interests and we knew she would be good at it, we both felt that the position wouldn't allow her to challenge herself and shine in the way that we knew she could. So, each of us put our foot down and told her not to take the position.

This was difficult for Siya. The company had made her a compelling offer and for good reason. She was bright, polished and talented and hiring her would have been a big victory for them. Shreyasi and I felt that a public policy position at the Albright Stonebridge Group (ASG) would be a much better fit for Siya. She would be working at a much higher level than in the other company and would have a much greater opportunity to grow.

After much back and forth, we finally won Siya over. She took the position at ASG and ended up thriving in that role. Looking back on it now, Siya cites our mentorship as one of the most significant moments of her career to date. She is grateful to have had people in her life who could peer below the surface of a situation that seemed quite obvious to her and point her towards a new direction.

This is one of the most essential aspects of mentorship. None of us can be perfectly objective about ourselves or the world around us. So, if we always try to go at it alone and make decisions without any input from others, we can often go astray. We need to be able to rely on other people who are invested in our success and have relatively more experience than we do, to uncover certain talents we didn't even know existed and point us in directions we didn't know were possible.

SIDEBAR: Institutional Mentorship Programmes

As the benefits of mentorship have become more popularized, there has been a growing demand to establish mentoring programmes in companies and academic institutions around the world. Cultivating talent is one of the most important elements of a company's long-term success and developing formal mentorship structures is a great way to facilitate this. According to a 2022 study by mentorcliQ, 84 per cent of US Fortune 500 companies have mentoring programmes and that number goes up to 100 per cent for Fortune 50 companies.[5]

Academic institutions are following this corporate trend. Here in India, for example, many prestigious law schools have started mentoring programmes in recent years, including the Bennett University School of Law, VIT School of Law, Lloyd Law College and IFIM Law School.[6]

These mentorship programmes can take many forms, including:

- **Internal vs external.** Some organizations choose to work with their HR departments to establish mentorship programmes using personnel within their organizations. Others will outsource the mentorship function, bringing in consultants or companies to mentor their employees.
- **Group programmes.** Many mentoring programmes are structured around peer groups. These groups often include a senior mentor who works with everyone collectively and individually. Groups are

often organized around department, function, or age
group and help to create a shared experience.

- **Online mentoring.** The internet has dramatically
expanded the opportunities for mentorship by
allowing for virtual meetings and check-ins. Mentors
and mentees no longer have to be in the same office
or country to engage with each other.
- **Peer-to-peer.** While there is a tremendous benefit to
being mentored by someone with more experience
than you, having a peer mentor can also be valuable.
Peer mentors can provide objectivity and a sense of
camaraderie and shared experience.

Holding You to a Higher Standard

There are many forms of mentorship. In some situations,
mentors find you. In other situations, you seek them out.
There are formal mentorship programmes, but some of
the most powerful mentorship, in fact, happens through
natural workplace collaboration. In cases like these,
more junior employees or students are working directly
with their seniors and have a tremendous opportunity to
learn by example. Mentors, in these cases, are essentially
teaching by doing.

It's in these interactions that you can experience one
of the most powerful benefits of mentorship: holding you
to a higher standard. For both Siya Sood and Monica
Hariharan, they experienced the power of this kind of
mentorship first hand through their work at the Albright
Stonebridge Group. While neither of them worked with
ASG at the same time, nor did they have the same job,

both talked about how much they learned by the intimate working environment of the company.

This isn't by accident. The work culture of ASG is such that lower-level employees like Monica and Siya work directly with the most senior executives in the company on virtually all projects. As a result, there is a great deal of learning through example. Siya talks about how the high standards that her co-workers set for both her and themselves, forced her to jump to a whole new level of rigour in how she approached work. As Monica describes it, ASG had a 'culture of excellence' where everyone was expected to stretch, grow and always give their best. This wasn't just an expectation set by the company's leadership. They set this standard through their own example. And in doing so, offered a valuable kind of mentorship for everyone who worked for and with them.

In the beginning, Siya says, the high standard of excellence was something that she was always striving to uphold, but it was coming from outside of her. Being in such a small group, nothing fell through the cracks and that forced her to take more responsibility than she would have in a larger, more hierarchical situation. Over time, she began to internalize the high standards of the team and become a generator herself. This is a lesson and a habit that she has carried with her throughout the rest of her career.

Monica has had a similar experience, finding that it was her time at ASG that set the tone for how she expects herself and others to perform in every job she's had since. Striving to always attain such a high standard has also given her immense confidence in any situation she finds herself in. Regardless of her experience level or her familiarity with the work, she can gain the trust of her teammates by holding a personal and collective standard of excellence. She's finding this experience more relevant than ever in her new role as a senior member of a food delivery start-up. For the first time in her career, she has the ability to really shape and build the culture of an organization from the ground up; and she's striving to create the same standard of excellence at her new company as she learned at ASG.

That's the thing about mentorship. It's not a one-time thing. The lessons you gain from a good mentor stick with you. They become a part of you. And as you progress in your career, you want to share those same lessons (and new ones you've picked up along the way) with others.

Modelling New Pathways

Another important benefit of having mentors is that they can open your mind up to opportunities you weren't aware of or didn't think possible. As we have discussed at length in this book, the world is changing rapidly, and modern careers are becoming more and more non-linear and 'outside the box.' When I was leaving school, there seemed to be only a handful of career options for me, whereas today, the possibilities seem endless. We live in a world where a tech degree can get you a job in a more traditional company like Microsoft or Intel; but it can also get you a job for a 'unicorn' company like Uber, TikTok or Coinbase.

But with all these options available to us, we still need examples of people who have made it happen. We need to see people who are not very different from ourselves and who have figured out creative ways to build their careers. When Monica Hariharan came to the Young India Fellowship, for example, she knew that she wanted to make a social impact, but she was confused about how to do so. Through that programme, she was able to connect directly with a wide variety of conscious entrepreneurs, activists and academics, who were tackling social issues in unique and novel ways. It opened up her mind to what was possible and allowed her to move forward on a path that was at once morally fulfilling, but also personally enjoyable.

Mentors can be these role models. They can show you how someone else did it and give you a very concrete example of what a career looks like. As human beings, we need these pathways ahead of us. Even if we don't follow them exactly, they give us somewhere to start. They give us the confidence that it's possible to build a career out of doing something you love.

Perhaps the most significant benefit to having a mentor is that they can give you the confidence to make a transition, even when you are fearful of the outcome. They can see the potential in an opportunity that's just not visible to you. And in doing so, they can help you cut through any ambivalence or indecision about your future. In our non-linear modern working world, where most of us will be faced with many important pivots along the way, having that kind of support and guidance proves to be invaluable.

This was certainly the case for me when Don Jacobs encouraged me to take a leap of faith and accept the ISB job. Indra Nooyi recounted a similar experience when her mentor supported her instincts to put her career on hold and get an MBA. Siya benefited greatly from the perspective that Shreyasi and I were able to provide at a rather critical moment. I am fortunate to have been able to pay this mentorship forward many times with the young people I've worked with over the years.

SIDEBAR: Closing the Skill Gap through Mentorship

Much has been written about the skill gap that many employers are experiencing, particularly with their younger millennial and Gen Z workers. Companies have been scrambling for over a decade to figure out how to understand and groom a new generation of workers to become valuable contributors to their workforce. One of the driving forces behind the skill gap has been the lack of efficient knowledge transfer between the older management and newer hires. This has been particularly difficult with soft skills like communication, leadership and collaboration.

One promising solution has been mentorship. According to a 2021 study published in the *International Journal of Evidence Based Coaching and Mentoring*, mentorship has had a strong impact on job performance among millennial workers, who currently make up roughly 50 per cent of the Indian workforce—a number that will rise to 75 per cent by 2025.[7]

Within Generation Z, research has shown that they are turning towards workplace supervisors as the primary mentors in their lives and away from other sources like coaches, teachers or religious leaders, which have been popular for older generations.[8] In fact, many employers are beginning to find that Gen Z workers respond better to mentorship than they do to management. In other words, they want to be nurtured and supported in their professional careers as opposed to micromanaged or told what to do.[9]

Finding a Mentor

As we conclude the chapter, you might be thinking, 'Okay, I get that mentorship is important, but how do I go about finding a mentor?' My simple answer to that question is that you're in luck. We are all literally surrounded by potential mentors. A mentor doesn't necessarily need to be someone you formally hire or ask to mentor you. It can be a parent or relative. It can be a teacher or academic advisor. It can be a boss or co-worker. It can be a member of an organization you volunteer for. It can be a coach or music instructor.

The thing about mentors is that as much as we seek them out, they often find us. That's the way it's worked for most of my career. When I find myself in a situation where I need some guidance, there is someone in my life that I feel naturally drawn to for advice. Of course, this isn't the case for everyone. But before you 'google' mentors, I suggest thinking about the relationships you already have as a source of mentorship. You might be surprised by how much support is readily available at your fingertips.

That said, there are plenty of formal mentoring programmes as well. If those appeal to you, I strongly suggest you seek them out. These could be programmes at your place of employment or school. If you're very clear about what you want mentoring for, you can hire someone like a coach to help you work through it. The key is that you have to take action to seek a mentoring relationship, whether it's with someone that's already in your life or not.

Oftentimes, when confronted with the possibility of mentorship, people respond by saying that they don't want to be an imposition or they don't think potential mentors would have time to help them out. But I've found that it's quite the opposite. There is a tremendous amount of goodwill in the world and mentors benefit as much (or more) from being able to share their experiences and wisdom to those they are helping out. That's the beauty of mentorship. It's often an act of pure goodwill and altruism. It's coming from someone's genuine desire to help you out coupled with your own willingness to listen and grow.

Exercises

Below you'll find some exercises you can use to help you cultivate mentorship relationships in your own life. You don't need to complete all of them, nor do you need to do them in any particular order. The key is to use them in any way that you think will benefit you most.

1. Who are your current mentors? Remember, these don't have to be formal mentorship relationships. It can be a relative, a coach, a teacher, or your boss. Who are the people you turn to for advice?

2. Think of the person or people you listed. What qualities and characteristics make them a good mentor?

3. Who might serve as future mentors for you? This could be someone in your life that you've never gone to for advice, but that you think could be a good source in the future.

4. If you were to reach out to a mentor (real or hypothetical) today, what would you ask them? Are there any issues you're seeking advice for?

5. Think of your answers in the question above. Who might be a good person to talk to about the topics that came to mind?

Advice for Parents: Tapping into the Secret Sauce

The world has changed significantly over the past three decades and nowhere has that transformation been as dramatic as in India. In essentially one generation, India has gone from a fairly isolated, backwater nation, to a major player in the global economy. When I graduated from IIT in the 1980s, India was just beginning to liberalize its economy and was far from the tiger it is today. While the total GDP in 1980 was below $200 billion, that number has exploded to nearly $3 trillion.[1] And this trend is likely to continue.

As a result of this rapid change, the workplace that Indian students are entering today is profoundly different from the one their parents faced only twenty or thirty years ago. There are far more educational and professional opportunities than there were when my generation was coming up. Not only do most major multinational corporations now have a presence in India, but the internet and its transoceanic fibre optic cables have, as

Thomas Freidman said, 'made the world flat' and allowed us to work directly with people and organizations around the globe.[2] Gone are the days when fresh graduates had only a few professions to choose from. There are so many new jobs and careers available today and these will only grow as we move into the future.

In light of all this transformation, the pace of change in our cultural institutions has, understandably, lagged behind our economic change. In many ways, the way we see the world has yet to catch up with how the world actually is. We see this cultural gap in many areas of modern life, but perhaps nowhere is it as prominent as in parenting—the ways in which we raise our children and the guidance we provide them as they look towards their future.

Parents today are faced with a unique generational conundrum. The world has changed so much and so fast during our adulthood that the disconnect between our experience and that of our children may be greater than at any other time in history. This means that we must be extremely careful not to project our own life experience onto those of our children. What worked for us—and worked extremely well in many cases——won't necessarily work for our children.

This doesn't mean that none of our life experiences or advice are relevant to our children. Quite to the contrary. It is crucial that we share many values that allowed us to thrive in our lives. But we must do so with an understanding that things are different today. We need to issue our advice with humility and an open mind. We have to find ways to translate our experiences into the language of the brave new world our children find themselves in.

That's what this chapter is all about. I asked each person I interviewed for the book to offer the best advice they have for parents today as they help their children to navigate the transition into adulthood and distilled their answers into a series of key points. Just as their life experience ranges the gamut of early professionals to retirees, their advice reflects a wide range of perspectives on parenting. The younger interviewees like Siya and Monica, who don't yet have children of their own, spoke more about the things that their own parents did or didn't do to help them navigate the modern workplace. The older interviewees who have children offered reflections based on their own parenting experience.

While this chapter is primarily written for parents, it can also be a useful tool for young people in a couple of ways. First off, the chapter can be a useful tool to share with your own parents as a conversation starter about your future. It might help you articulate thoughts that are difficult for you to share with them. It might inspire them to think differently about their expectations of what you are or will be doing with your own education and career.

This chapter can also be beneficial to non-parents, because it provides a unique twist on many of the principles we've already explored in the book. We've gone into great detail about some of the key ingredients for getting started on a successful career in a time when everything is changing so quickly and looking at these ingredients from the perspective of a parent can help to enrich your understanding of the material.

Regardless of where you are on the parent to child spectrum, I encourage you to approach this chapter with an open mind. All of the advice I share is not meant to convince you or shame you into changing your ways. It's meant to offer some new insights and perspectives that can expand your own view of the world and what is possible for you and your children.

SIDEBAR: Are We Pressuring Our Kids Too Much?

While the cultural pressure to succeed is by no means unique to India, it may be higher in this country than many throughout the world. This, of course, can have a damaging effect on the freedom young people feel to pursue careers that they are best suited for. But the high degree of pressure that kids feel to succeed in school may also be taking a toll on their mental health, and in the most extreme cases, causing a rise in suicides. According to the National Crime Records Bureau, twenty-eight students commit suicide every day and the total number of student suicides as of 2018 was 26 per cent higher than it was a decade earlier. [3]

There are, of course, many factors driving this alarming trend, but the pressure students feel to perform in school is likely a prominent one. One piece of evidence that school pressure is a contributing factor is the high number of suicides occurring at elite preparatory schools. According to the Department of Higher Education, twenty-seven students attending various IITs committed suicide between 2014 and 2019. And in Kota, which is home to many elite coaching programmes, fifty-eight students have committed suicide between 2013 and 2017.[4]

I don't cite these statistics to be an alarmist. Nor am I suggesting that by encouraging kids to apply themselves to their education, we are forcing them into suicide. But they do represent one alarming symptom of an educational system that doesn't present our kids with the proper encouragement or support to develop in ways that are not only healthy, but also more conducive to success in the modern professional marketplace.

The Room to Experiment

As we've discussed at great length in this book, there is a tremendous amount of pressure for young people to make decisions about their future at very young ages. For example, when they hit grade eleven in high school, they'll be asked to decide whether they should take the science or humanities track. Next, they'll have a choice of what college or university to attend and what they should major in. The same will happen with graduate school and early job choices.

Every step of the way, you as a parent will have a significant influence over their choices. And perhaps more than anything else you do as a parent, it's crucial that you let them know that it's okay for them to be confused about which direction to take. As we've laid out in the book, it's nearly impossible for someone to know exactly what they want to do in their future at such an early age; and even if they do, the world is changing so fast that such rare clarity is really more of an educated guess.

So, one of the best gifts you can give them as a parent is the room to experiment. It's okay, for example, if your child doesn't know if they prefer sciences or humanities when they are only seventeen years old. If they're not clear, you can help them make their best guess about which track to take, without putting any kind of pressure on them. Let them know that they can always change their mind. And don't place too much value on their past educational experiences. If they say they 'hate math,' for example, it might have as much to do with having a bad teacher as it does to do with a natural distaste. They can always come back to a subject later in their studies. It doesn't all have to happen upfront.

When it comes to choosing a college and a major, it's important for you to help take the pressure off to make the perfect choice. As we discussed in Chapter 3, it's far more imperative for students to get into the best possible school than it is to choose the perfect major. The reputation of their school will likely open up more doors in the future than the specific major they choose. Focus more on the quality of the institution and make sure that there are diverse academic programmes that they can explore. Again, it's okay for them to not be clear. They will figure it out eventually, so you want to give them the best educational environment to support that kind of flexibility.

Through all of this, it's crucial that you, as a parent, let your children know that it's okay to 'not know.' They are under enough pressure from society as it is. They'll likely look around at their peers and assume that everyone else has it figured out and there's something wrong with them if they haven't. You need to be a source of the opposite view in their lives. Let them know that they have plenty of time to figure out what they want to do and that they don't have to worry about making the perfect choice. It's the truth after all. We live in a dynamic, ever-changing world where uncertainty is the norm. Helping them cultivate this mindset from a young age will be critical to their long-term success.

They're Different from You

One of the biggest pieces of advice that the interviewees shared is that it's paramount for parents to remember that their children are different from them. As we discussed in the previous section, the world is very different from how it was twenty or thirty years ago and so is the younger generation. They've been shaped by a completely different world than you have. They want different things for their lives. Their values are considerably different. As 'digital natives,' they were raised with the global-connectedness that the internet has enabled. They live on social media and are more aware of what's going on in the distant corners of the globe than ever before. As parents, we need to acknowledge and learn about these differences in order for our guidance to be relevant and effective.

One of the biggest changes we're seeing in the younger generations today is around social awareness. And as Nikhil Sud pointed out, it's crucial for parents to understand that many of their children's decisions are being driven by ethical and social concerns, sometimes even more than a desire for personal success. Millennials and Generation Z are perhaps the most socially conscious generations in history. And that's especially true here in India. The Deloitte 2021 millennial and Gen Z Survey, found that among young people in India, personal beliefs are more influential over the kinds of careers they choose (72 per cent for millennials and 66 per cent for Gen Z) than the global average (44 per cent for millennials and 49 per cent for Gen Z).[5] This emphasis on ethics-based work makes sense. Not only have the internet and social media made us more aware of the global impacts of our personal choices, but we are also facing major global challenges like never before, from climate change to the COVID-19 pandemic.

Nikhil suggests another social area where views have changed is around LGBTQ+ issues, which are often a major sticking point within Indian families, partly because older generations tend to be far more conservative than their children. While India trends progressive on many issues, when it comes to issues like sexual orientation and gender identity, we still lag behind. Things are looking better each day with certain sections of the younger Indian population starting to influence the narrative on these issues, but much work remains. This is a country, after all, where same-sex relationships were only decriminalized by the Indian Supreme Court in 2018. Nikhil believes that the country's lingering conservative tendencies on these issues often contribute to young Indians' decisions to study and live abroad in countries with more liberal views—even Indians who do not belong to the LGBTQ+ community but see the importance of such issues.

The significance of mental health is also an emerging value among younger generations. Whereas things like going to therapy were relatively a taboo in my generation, they are becoming commonplace among millennials and Gen Z. As Nikhil points out, within the last decade, views about mental health in Indian society have begun to change. Many attribute this partly to Bollywood star Deepika Padukone speaking publicly about her struggles with depression in 2015, which opened up a broader cultural conversation around mental health and empowered many people to be transparent about their own issues.[6] Mental health is a particularly pressing issue for parents to be aware of with their children. They need to feel supported and able to speak with you about any issues they may be struggling with.

The good news about these generational differences is that they're easy to tackle within your own family. But as Nikhil suggests, it requires you to have an open mind. He describes many value clashes as simply 'mental blocks' that, if you're willing to talk about, often end up being less divisive than you might expect. The key is to give your children the space to be who they are as they navigate some of the biggest decisions they've faced in their young lives. Remember that while you have helped to shape who they are, they may be quite different from you in some important ways. Your children need to know that these differences are okay, in order for them to have the confidence and freedom to chart their future effectively.

Help Them Figure Out What They Love

When I asked the interviewees for the book to give me their best advice for parents, there was one response that stood out above the others. Nearly all of them gave me some version of the same story. Reflecting on the early years of their own lives and careers, they wished they would have been given more time and opportunity to think about what they really wanted to do with their lives, rather than just what might be the most successful path. And they suggested that one of the most important things parents can do to help prepare their children for the modern workplace is to help them discover what they love and what they're good at.

As we discussed in Chapter 1, one of the key contentions of this book is that it's possible to build a successful career doing something you love. At the same time, the various forms of the 'do something you love' advice tends to be quite misleading as they don't really tell you *how* to do it, only that it's possible. It's similar for the parenting advice around this topic. As a parent, it's not enough to simply say 'find your passion.' This can often backfire, especially if young people don't really know themselves yet. They might conclude that there's something wrong with them. So, the best role you can play as a parent is to help them discover themselves, gradually and without any pressure to figure it out quickly.

Siya Sood had some particularly concrete advice for how parents can help their children to better discover their passions. First off, she suggests that parents should avoid becoming overly concerned with grades. Grades, she admits, are important, especially if you want to get into a good school. It's just that you shouldn't think that getting good grades will ensure your successful future. Rather, she suggests that having a well-rounded base of experiences and skills to draw from will serve you better in the long run.

Another pertinent piece of advice she offered was for parents to get actively involved in helping their kids to experiment with different experiences so they can begin to identify and learn what they like and what they are good at. There are so many opportunities to do this. Support their hobbies. 'If you're going to pay for a math tutor,' she says, 'why not also pay for guitar lessons?' Remember, being well-rounded and having a range of skill sets is more crucial to their long-term success than simply excelling in school or in their exams. As they move deeper into their education, you can also encourage them to get internships and use any connections you or your family might have to get them. Internships are great opportunities for young people to experiment with different career paths and learn about what they like and are good at through real-world experiences.

Finally, Siya suggests that parents do their best to learn about how the world is changing. Her parents, for example, weren't well-versed in the job opportunities available to her. Her father ran a family legacy business and her mother worked in a small city. They didn't know enough about the modern job world to be able to effectively guide her in one direction or another. If parents can make the effort to expose themselves to the diversity of opportunities available today, they're more likely to help their children cultivate a wider array of skills and experiences, which will serve them better in times to come. This might take the form of staying with the current trends and reading about up-and-coming entrepreneurs in business media. It could also include attending talks at local educational institutions.

Prepare Them, Don't Instruct Them

When I asked Nikhil for his best advice for parents, his answer was particularly insightful. He made the point that parents need to first ask themselves whether they actually have the requisite experience or knowledge to effectively guide their children. 'In order to be good mentors to their children,' he said, 'they need to determine if they know enough about the world that their children are about to enter.' For example, if their child is thinking about going abroad for school, they need to ask themselves if they know enough about that experience to effectively advise them.

For Nikhil, it is more important for parents to prepare their children to be able to navigate difficult decisions, rather than instructing them on the particulars, especially in areas where parents are not well-versed. For example, if your child comes to you for advice about whether or not to take a job they have been offered, rather than giving your opinion on which is best, you can help them to ask the right kind of questions in order to come to an answer themselves. He credits his own parents with taking this kind of approach with him. When he would approach them on an issue they were somewhat unfamiliar with, they would try to become familiar with it. Then if that wasn't practicable, they'd challenge him only on the rigour of the thinking he undertook to reach his conclusion rather than on the actual outcome of the decision.

Srikant Sastri calls this approach to parenting 'guidance with a light touch,' and it's one that he's employed with both of his two adult children and with the many young entrepreneurs that he has mentored over the years. In his view, there's a fine balance between stepping in and giving young people advice and letting them figure things out for themselves. If you fall too heavily on either side of this equation it could backfire. Young people will either tune you out completely or blindly take your advice without learning how to think through a difficult decision.

Like Nikhil, Srikant believes the best advice focuses on the process of making decisions rather than the decisions themselves. He's a big advocate of teaching young people how to approach a big decision in their lives: how to break it down into its component parts, how to weigh the pros and cons, how to think through all the potential outcomes and how to ask all the right questions. He's found that when you approach advice this way, it tends to have more of a lasting impact than just telling people what to do. You're teaching them how to think, not what to think. And that's a skill they can carry with them moving forward. It's a variation on the old saying, 'If you give a person a fish, they'll eat for a day. If you teach them how to fish, they'll eat for a lifetime.'

Of course, there are always times when you, as a parent, need to be more heavy-handed in your guidance.

You don't want your children making catastrophic mistakes or blunders that will damage them in the present or future. And they are young, after all, with very little life experience to draw upon. So, you have to find a way to be balanced in your approach. Finding the right moments to be stronger in your guidance and when to step back and let them figure things out on their own.

Siya credits her parents' version of 'light-touch guidance' with giving her a tremendous amount of confidence at an early age. Siya's parents didn't put an incredible amount of pressure on her when she was young, even when she slacked off in school and at times seemed wayward. As a result, she experiences much less anxiety than many of her peers. She had a kind of innate sense that everything would be okay. Her parents allowed her to learn from her mistakes and had confidence that she would eventually find her way. And she did.

Building Agility and Resilience

In my experience, the two most crucial qualities young people need to successfully navigate the ever-changing modern career paths they will likely face in their future are agility and resilience. Agility is the ability to adapt and evolve as the world around you perpetually undergoes change. Resilience is its close cousin and is essentially the capacity to overcome setbacks and bounce back from them stronger and more able. And while there are many skills and experiences that you may not be well-equipped to provide your children, helping them to develop agility and resilience is well within your control. In fact, helping your children to cultivate these two qualities may be the most important thing you do for them as a parent.

Why? In a world of constant change, those of us who are able to adapt quickly and recover from setbacks will have a distinct advantage over those who are stuck in their ways and can't deal with failure. The world simply isn't a static entity. It's dynamic and unpredictable. It throws you curveballs more than fastballs. It pushes you to juggle with uncomfortable situations. So, young people need to be comfortable in this chaotic environment. They actually need to embrace it.

The question is, how do you as a parent help your children develop the agility and resilience necessary to thrive?

When it comes to helping your children develop agility, the key is diversity—in their skills, in their experiences and in the environment they're exposed to. As we discussed in Chapter 4, it's essential to have as wide an array of skills as possible that you can draw on in the multitude of situations you find yourself in. To use a visual metaphor, imagine that your child is a kind of handyman (or woman) and their squiggly career is a household they've been asked to visit in order to make a series of repairs. In order to best prepare them for what they'll encounter in the house—a leaky faucet, a damaged air conditioning unit, or a termite infestation—they will need a wide variety of tools in their toolkit. So, one of your jobs, as a parent, is to encourage them to have the most diverse toolkit available.

So rather than forcing them down the often-trod, narrow path that so many students take, encourage your children to try new things—and support them thereafter. As Siya suggested earlier in the chapter, diversifying your child's experiences could include things like supporting hobbies and internships, but there are innumerable ways to do this. It could also be as simple as giving your child new jobs around the house, as my father did for me, to teach them how to do a wide variety of things. The key is to be proactive and creative. Don't force your children to do a lot of things. Rather, encourage them to try experiences you think might be relevant. And support them when they express their own interests.

The obvious benefit of helping to diversify your child's toolkit is that they'll have many more skills and experiences to draw on when they are presented with a situation that demands change and evolution. They'll be more agile in their ability to tread a new path because they'll have a deeper reservoir to dip into. Take the example of Steve Jobs from Chapter 5. He talks about how taking a random calligraphy class in college eventually ended up coming in handy when he developed the typography for the first Apple computer. The more diverse your skills, the more ways you'll be able to adapt to the changing landscape of your future.

But there's another, less obvious way that having a diversity of skills and experiences contributes to agility. When you encounter new situations, whether that be a class on public speaking or an internship with a local government official, you learn how to learn. Every time you find yourself at the starting line of a new endeavour, you start a new learning cycle. You get more practice learning and, in the process, you become a better learner.

This could take the form of learning a new specialty. In Chapter 4, for example, we talked about how one of the key things I gained from the experience of getting my PhD in robotics was learning how to become a specialist in a particular field. I then applied many of those very learning skills in a wide variety of situations throughout my career. Learning how to learn made me more agile.

A friend of mine recently shared with me his experience of a different kind of agility, which he calls 'cultural agility.' When he was a child, his parents' work required that they move frequently and to different cities in diverse regions around the country. That meant that he and his sister were constantly starting over—changing schools, making new friends and learning to navigate the new cultures in each city they moved to. At the time, he didn't like having to move. But looking back, he says that it gave him a unique kind of agility. He became adept at developing relationships quickly, adapting to different cultural worldviews and was comfortable in foreign environments. This cultural agility has benefitted him greatly in his life and career.

On the flip side of agility is resilience. Resilience is a complex quality. It includes the ability to bounce back and learn from setbacks. It includes having the emotional strength to withstand difficult situations without falling apart. And perhaps most importantly, it includes becoming comfortable with failure.

As a parent, one of the most vital things you can do to prepare your child for their future is helping them to fail. Let me explain. All of us will encounter a great deal of failure in our lives, especially if we are growing and taking risks. For example, it's common for successful entrepreneurs to cite their early failures as crucial to their eventual success. Failing and then learning from that failure is one of the most important skills we all need to master to succeed.

So as a parent, you need to give your children the opportunity to fail, especially early in their lives. This could seem challenging and difficult. Parents tend to do everything they can to help their children avoid failure. Why on earth would you let your child fail when one of your primary responsibilities as a parent is to ensure and safeguard their success? Sometimes long-term success requires having an early taste of failure. If you give your children the chance to fail and then learn from it, early in their lives, they'll be better prepared for the inevitable failures they will experience down the line. They'll be more comfortable with failure.

So how do you do this? The first step is to overcome your own fear of failure. As we discussed in Chapter 5, the less you're afraid to fail, the better prepared you'll be when things don't go your way. If you can embrace this in your own life, you'll be a model for your children. You'll show them that it's okay not to be perfect. You'll be an example of someone who takes risks, even when there's a strong chance that you won't succeed.

The next step in helping your children to become better at failing, is encouraging them to take on big challenges. Try a new instrument. Apply for a challenging school. Learn a new language. Start a business. You should support your children in biting off more than they can chew, so they can feel what it's like for them to fail. They need to have a direct experience of the disappointment that comes with failure, so they can learn that the feeling is fleeting. It's not nearly as big a deal as they perceive it to be.

Finally, you need to actually let them fail in ways that won't jeopardize their future. For example, in order for your child to learn a lesson about the hard work required for success, you might need to let them fail a test or get eliminated from a team. This way, they'll experience the consequences directly themselves and be in a position to learn a valuable lesson for how to approach things differently in the future. Rather than cushioning from the hard lessons of life, let them learn from their own experience.

This is the hardest step as a parent, because it goes against all your instincts. The good news is that when your children are young, the failures they experience under your watchful guidance won't be as damaging. They won't really be failing in the long run if you are there to help them learn from their mistakes. In this way, you can help them run a kind of controlled experiment with their life. They can take risks in an environment where failure won't be as catastrophic. This way, they can build resilience gradually and organically.

SIDEBAR: The Indian Advantage

Over the past half century, India and its citizens, both domestic and abroad, have developed a reputation for being some of the most hardworking and successful people on earth. Not only have we been one of the world's fastest growing economies for decades, but Indians who emigrate to other countries have thrived.

The strength of the Indian diaspora is particularly distinct in America. In their 2019 book, *The Other One Percent: Indians in America*, professors Sanjoy Chakravorty, Devesh Kapur and Nirvikar Singh lay out an impressive array of statistics showing the many ways that Indian Americans have overachieved relative to American society as a whole. For example, Indians make up 8 per cent of the founders of high-tech companies and one-third of Silicon Valley tech start-ups, even though they comprise less than 1 per cent of the US population as a whole. Sixty-eight per cent of Indian-born citizens have college degrees and their average incomes are generally higher than those associated with their level of education.[7]

What's behind this Indian edge? Many have suggested that our national obsession with education has driven this global achievement. Demographically speaking, 35 per cent of India's billion people population is under the age of thirty-five. This young, ambitious population has created a tremendous demand for education. As a result, there simply aren't enough high-quality institutions within the country to meet this demand. This is one of the reasons so many choose to study abroad. This supply-and-demand issue has also created extremely high competition within India's top universities, which have remarkably high standards and lower acceptance rates than American Ivy League schools. The challenge of getting into them and then thriving in the Indian higher educational system has, in many ways, driven the character and work ethic of those who make it through. There is a tremendous toughness, grit and determination among young Indians that many believe at least partially explains our global success.[8]

The Secret Sauce

When I asked Monica Hariharan to offer the best advice for today's parents, her eyes lit up. Monica doesn't have children of her own, but she has a host of opinions on the subject, which she shared with me enthusiastically. And despite the fact that she's not a parent, she offered what may have been the most sage advice I encountered in my research for the book.

In Monica's view, parents today have a monumental task. They have to instill in their children the values that helped them to succeed, but do it in a manner that doesn't project their own worldview, which was shaped in a different era. Indians, generally speaking, have developed an international reputation for being among the smartest, most hardworking and resourceful people on earth. This success, Monica suggests, has been largely due to the values, ethics and character of the Indian culture. It's what drove my generation to spark the incredible growth of the Indian economy over the past thirty years. It's also behind the remarkable success of the Indian diaspora in countries around the world.

Monica believes that the secret sauce for everyone looking to succeed in today's world is to take all of those deeper values and find new ways to express them. Parents, for example, can teach their children the hard work and dedication they used to succeed as doctors and engineers, but let their children find new professions in which to apply them. They can encourage their children to strive for excellence in new ways that are relevant to the world we live in now. Young people can express the dependability and integrity of previous generations through opportunities that weren't available to their parents.

I couldn't agree more with Monica's assessment and believe that the secret sauce that we—as parents and mentors—have to offer the next generation is this deeper set of values. It's a kind of ethical template for success that the next generation can apply freely and creatively in the brave new world we are living in. That template is defined by hard work, excellence, rigorous thinking, dependability, resilience and adaptability. The key for parents today is to give their children this template without being too prescriptive in how to apply it. Learn to let go and trust that all the wisdom and character you've inculcated will lead to new and surprising successes in the lives they architect for themselves.

Exercises

The exercises for this chapter are a little different than in the others. I've broken them up into two categories: a set for parents and a set for students, or young people. If your primary reason for reading this book is helping to prepare your kids for the future, then use the first set of questions. If you're reading this book to help you prepare yourself, then use the second set. If it's both, then feel free to complete all of them.

For Parents:

1. What are your greatest fears and anxieties about your children's future? Write them down and contemplate each of them. Are these fears fully valid? Are there ways in which your view is limited or biased by your own past?
2. Think about your child or children. What are they passionate about? What are they good at?
3. Look at your answers to the question above. What have you done to help your child cultivate these aptitudes and interests? Is there anything more you could be doing?
4. Reflect on your own professional journey. Were there interests that you wish you had been able to pursue in your career? If you didn't, what held you back? What could you do for your own children that your parents didn't do for you?
5. Schedule a meeting with your child or children and go through the answers you came to above.

For Students:

1. What would you say are the key expectations that your parents have for you, in the present and the future? Are these the same expectations you have for yourself? Why or why not?
2. Consider the various parenting principles outlined in this chapter. Think about your own parents and reflect on how well they are doing on each of them. For example, do you feel they give you guidance with

a light touch? Do they help you to cultivate agility and resilience? Why or why not?

3. What role have mentors beyond your parents played in your life? Are there qualities they possess that you wish your parents embodied?

4. After reading this chapter, do you feel as if you have a better understanding of your parents and your relationship with them? Why or why not?

5. Schedule a meeting with your parents to talk about your answers to the questions above.

Conclusion

Unlocking a Growth Mindset

In his 2022 commencement speech at Cape Cod Community College in Massachusetts, Netflix co-founder Marc Randolph made a controversial statement to the hundreds of students, faculty and family members in attendance. He said that 'follow your dreams' might be the worst thing to tell young people, even though it is 'the most dispensed advice in the history of mankind.'

Why?

Randolph continued, 'It's not the advice itself that's bad. It's bad because all the well-meaning people telling you to follow your dreams leave out something important. They never tell you how.' Instead, he advocates that young people should 'stop thinking [and] start doing.' He believes it's more crucial to learn how to execute your goals so that when you do discover your 'dreams,' whatever they may be, you'll be in a position to practically make them come true.[1]

In my experience, Randolph's estimation of this perennial advice for idealistic young people is spot on.

While I'm a big believer in the fact that it is truly possible to build a career of your dreams, just *saying* it's possible can't really help you make it a reality. And, as we've discussed at great length in this book, most of us aren't clear enough about our dreams when we're young to follow them.

The reason people never tell you *how* to follow your dreams isn't because they're ignorant or don't know what they're talking about. It's because the 'how' is impossible to define in specific terms, especially in our rapidly changing world. The pathways ahead of us are just too hard-to-predict and squiggly. And each of us is unique. Our dreams are different and so are the rates at which we discover them. Some of us know early on what we want to do, but most of us figure it out through experimentation and action. So, it's pretty difficult—impossible, really—to tell someone exactly 'how' to follow their dreams.

I believe that we should update this perennial advice for the twenty-first century. Instead of telling people to 'follow your dreams,' we should say 'discover your dreams.' This flips the concept on its head. Your dreams, from this vantage point, aren't some fixed entities that you need to simply define and then follow. They are dynamic and changing. They are something to be discovered through the process of your own career journey. Discovering your dreams requires experimentation and testing. It requires throwing yourself into new situations and over time, figuring out what you are best at and what gives you the most sense of fulfillment.

A Mindset for Growth

When you make the shift from seeing your dreams as something to follow to something you discover, you are, in essence, assuming what has come to be known as a 'growth mindset.' You've likely heard this term referred to in a personal development book, career blog or TED Talk. In fact, the idea of having a growth mindset has become quite popular in many circles; and for good reason.

First popularized by Stanford University Psychology Professor Carol Dweck in her 2007 book, *Mindset: The New Psychology of Success*, the concept of a growth mindset is based on the recognition that there is nothing about us that is static. Who we are, what we're good (or bad) at, what we want to do with our lives—all have the potential to change and develop over time. We are not limited or fixed entities. We can evolve and grow.

The genius of the work that Dweck and others have done to define the growth vs fixed mindset is that they've unlocked a kind of psychological 'secret' that was hiding in plain sight—one that holds so many of us back from achieving our potential. Whether we're aware of it or not, most of us start out with the opposite of a growth mindset. We unconsciously believe that who we are is static and unchanging. And synonymous with this belief is an assumption that our future success will be determined not by effort or will, but by our God-given talents (or lack thereof). If we are fixed, then we can't grow. So why even bother trying.[2]

But that's the beauty of the growth mindset. It's based on the actual reality of the world we're living in—a world defined by constant change and opportunity. It's an understanding that we are all 'a work in progress' and that by applying effort and ingenuity to our lives, we can become better. This orientation creates a solid psychological foundation for navigating the squiggly careers that most of us have or will have in this day and age. In many ways, all of the people interviewed in this book have been driven by some degree of a growth mindset throughout their careers. And the principles we've explored together all represent different reflections of a growth mindset.

We've talked about the importance of self-discovery and how this is something that happens gradually over time and with ample experience. The fixed view on this topic is the one we most commonly encounter: that you need to figure out your passions and talents early so you can start the process of focusing on them. But as so many people that we've met over the course of this book can attest the fact that it just doesn't work like that for most of us. We learn about our passions and talents over time through experimentation and experiences. They are not fixed, but perpetually growing and changing.

We've also talked about the importance of developing a wide range of skills, especially deeper skills, in order to have the agility to evolve and adapt over time. This kind of agility is key to a growth mindset because it gives you a diversity of tools to pivot when necessary. Additionally, the more skills, specialities and worldviews you encounter in your education, the more malleable your mind will be. The more perspectives you immerse yourself in, the less fixed your mind will be.

You'll be more open to different realities and that leaves you more open to growth.

If you see yourself as a growing and changing entity, you'll also be less afraid of failure. You'll be more willing to experiment with your life and career, try new experiences and learn as much as you can every step of the way. You won't think of your choices as 'wrong' or 'right,' but more as learning opportunities that give you the required information about what works and what doesn't. With a growth mindset, you'll want to pick up as many dots as you can, so you can eventually make the all-important connections between them—the connections that will ultimately define and propel your career.

From the vantage point of a growth mindset, you'll want to seek out as much mentorship as possible. You'll want to interact with others who push you to strive for more and better. You'll be willing to be more vulnerable with those you turn to for advice, because you won't be protecting some static idea of who you are. You'll want their guidance since you're more focused on who you want to become. The mere act of seeking mentorship is a powerful symptom of a growth mindset, as you have the humility to recognize that you don't have all the answers and need help to discover who you are meant to be.

As parents, modelling and encouraging a growth mindset for your children is crucial to their success. Just like you didn't expect them to be the same person at age thirteen as they were when they were age five, you shouldn't expect them to know who they will be at age forty when they are only sixteen years of age. Assuming a growth mindset in relationship to your children will enable you to prepare them for a world where they aren't afraid to fail and aren't overly concerned with choosing the perfect path. You'll help them to see themselves and their career as evolving entities. You'll be less focused on helping them to get it 'right,' and more focused on equipping them with the skills and tools they need to navigate the countless pivots they'll make in the future.

As you can see, cultivating a growth mindset is at the foundation of navigating the squiggly careers that most of us are having or are likely to have in our modern world. Following the examples and working with the principles we've explored thus far in the book will help you to do so.

SIDEBAR: Three Common Misconceptions about the Growth Mindset

Since the publication of *Mindset: A New Psychology of Success* in 2007, Carol Dweck has become renowned for her insights into how, for cultivating a growth mindset, one has to unlock individual potential in a wide variety of areas and disciplines. And the term 'growth mindset' has been adopted and used by millions of people around the world.

But Dweck is quick to point out that not everyone who endorses a growth mindset really knows what it means, or more importantly, how to achieve it. In a 2016 article for the *Harvard Business Review* entitled 'What Having a 'Growth Mindset' Actually Means,'[3] she identified three of the most common misconceptions about the principle:

1. **Having a growth mindset is the same as being open minded.** Dweck points out that many people confuse having a growth mindset with simply being positive or open-minded and then conclude that they must therefore be growth-oriented. By her definition, however, we are all a mixed bag of growth and fixed mindsets and can constantly improve in making ourselves more and more growth-oriented.

2. **A growth mindset should bear results.** Building a growth mindset isn't just about trying your best. Achieving outcomes matters as well. While everything can and should be an opportunity for growth, you can't fail all the time. You need to learn to accomplish your goals as part of the growth process.

3. **Getting a growth mindset is a one-time epiphany.** Many people make the mistake of getting aligned philosophically with a growth mindset and thinking that's enough to inspire them to embody it. But that just isn't the case. Putting a growth mindset into practice takes just that: practice. Like developing any new habit, it takes constant correction and reaffirmation.

The main premise running through all of these misconceptions is that cultivating a growth mindset is somehow easy or natural. But as Dweck points out, it just isn't. It takes work. We are wired to see ourselves and the world as fixed entities. It's our default setting. So, rewiring ourselves towards growth takes constant effort, trial and error. It's not a one-time thing, but a life-long endeavour.

Growth Embodied

As I've tried to do with every principle we've explored in this book, I want to show you what a growth mindset looks like in the real world through the lives of individuals I've interviewed. None of their careers perfectly reflect this orientation. That's just not possible. As Dweck has pointed out, cultivating and sustaining a growth mindset is a lifelong process of constant refinement.

There may be no better example of someone who embodied a growth mindset than Srikant Sastri, the serial entrepreneur whom we met in Chapter 6. Srikant was a contemporary of mine at IIT Kanpur, in the 1980s, but as he describes it, he 'lived a twenty-first-century life in the twentieth century.' From a very young age, he knew that he wanted to be an entrepreneur, even though at that time, entrepreneurship wasn't really an option for young people in India. Srikant wasn't clear about exactly what industry he would end up in, but he was compelled by the idea of growing businesses. He didn't come from a business family and had few examples to draw inspiration from, but he pursued the life of an entrepreneur in spite of all that. He didn't allow these cultural limitations to define his sense of what was possible for his life. He had to transcend his fixed mindset in order to open himself up to growth.

For Srikant, his entrepreneurial growth started by enrolling in an MBA programme after getting his undergraduate degree in engineering in order to gain some foundational experience with the principles of business, a move that went against the grain of what most of his peers did at the time. After completing graduate school, he took a job with Pond's (now part of Unilever) to learn the ropes of the business world within one of the most successful companies in the world. He then took a job in marketing, which he considered an essential skill to learn in order to be a successful entrepreneur.

At this point in his career, Srikant felt he was ready to make the leap and start his own company. But it was the early 1990s and there was little support in India for aspiring entrepreneurs. The economy was just starting to open up to foreign investment and there weren't a plethora of venture capitalists or start-up incubators that there are today. Even though he had been preparing for this leap for his whole career, Srikant had to take a big risk. As he recalls, 'Everyone thought I was crazy.' But he did it anyway, applying a growth mindset to focus more on what was possible than what already existed. He drew upon his professional experience to create a marketing company that multinational corporations in the medical and technology sectors could subcontract to do their work in India. The gamble paid off, and Srikant's company grew rapidly. By 2006, they had 3,000 staff across India and Southeast Asia.

But Srikant was getting bored. His desire for growth had reached its limits with the company and he wanted to create something new. He sold the company and started another venture, this time a contract staffing business that helped hire and train employees across Asia for companies like Hewlett Packard and Microsoft. Like his first company, the new venture was a success. By the time he sold it in 2010, the company had grown to include 15,000 employees.

At this point in his career, Srikant felt that after growing two different companies, he'd fulfilled his entrepreneurial dreams, but he didn't want to retire. He wasn't done learning and growing. He shifted into the educational side of business, acting as a consultant on exciting new ventures and serving as a mentor for aspiring entrepreneurs. As has been the case throughout his career, he remains focused on growth: of companies, of individuals and of his own diverse interests. Srikant is adamant in his belief that young people can achieve extraordinary things, even in hard-to-define arenas, if they are willing to keep their eyes constantly focused on growth and opportunity. He is passionate about continuing to evolve himself and inspiring others to cultivate a growth mindset of their own.

Of course, having a growth mindset doesn't only lead you to grow companies. It's something you can apply to any career path. Take Paroma Roy Chowdhury, for example. One of the superpowers that has driven her long and winding career has been her willingness to jump boldly into new opportunities that were well outside her comfort zone. As you may recall from her story in Chapter 5, Paroma leapt from journalism school into the first phase of her career working as an editor for various business newspapers and magazines, despite the fact that she had virtually no prior experience in any aspect of business. In doing so, Paroma was applying a critical element of the growth mindset: she didn't let her preconceived notions about who she was limit her from trying something new.

And this trend continued. Paroma then pivoted into the world of corporate communications, taking a job with

GE Capital. While she's remained in a similar role for the remainder of her career, she has continuously shifted into new industries, from information technology to EdTech. With each move, Paroma had to jump beyond any fixed sense of who she was, what she could accomplish, or what type of job or industry she was best suited for. As a result, she's continued to grow throughout her career and achieved things she could never have imagined when she started out.

A Lifelong Journey

In the commencement speech I referred to at the opening to this chapter, Marc Randolph didn't just talk about what advice not to heed ('follow your dreams'). He gave some new advice he believes is more relevant to the world we're living in today. His primary message is simple: chill. 'Whatever it is you want to do, you've got time. Don't worry about your career following a straight line . . . Uncertainty is exciting and I'm jealous because you have the whole world in front of you.'

I want to leave you with a similar nugget of wisdom. As you peer into your career, whether it be from the vantage point of a high school student, a college graduate, or a mid-career professional, it's imperative to do so with patience and curiosity. Don't fall victim to the pressure from your peers or teachers or family or society to prematurely figure it all out. If you're not certain about what you want to do with your life, that's okay. The world isn't certain, so how could you be?

As you take the first step or the next step in your career journey, try to see it as a learning opportunity. If you're facing a decision about which job to take, which school to attend or what to major in, do the necessary work to make the best choice possible, but don't fret over getting it perfectly right. I promise that it probably won't make or break your career. You can learn from every decision you make and you have plenty of time to try new things if your initial choice doesn't end up working out the way you wanted it to.

The truth is that your life is bound to have twists and turns—probably a lot of them. You might study software engineering and end up working in non-profit communications. Or you might get a degree in journalism and end up starting your own online food delivery business. You might decide to go back to school midway through your career. When I graduated from the IIT, I could never have imagined I would end up as a university founder and educational entrepreneur. Those opportunities were simply far beyond the horizon of who I was at the time. But it happened.

The point is your life is bound to change, multiple times and it's imperative that you welcome that change with open arms. Don't try to turn away from it. Expect it. Embrace it. Harness it. If you can see your life and career in this way and do your best to always orient towards growth and development, you'll be surprised at how far you'll reach. You'll defy the wildest expectations for your life and do things you would have never imagined yourself doing. And one day, you'll look back, connect the dots of your squiggly career and be amazed at how much you've achieved.

Exercises

Below are a series of exercises you can use to explore the concept of the growth mindset directly in your own life. Feel free to skip around and complete them in any order you prefer.

1. Reflect on the concept of having a fixed versus growth mindset in your own life. Can you identify any key choices you've made that reflect a fixed mindset? How could your choices have been different if you had approached them with more of a growth orientation?

2. Can you identify any experiences or decisions in your life that you approached with a growth mindset? What were the outcomes? What did you learn from those experiences?

3. Try the following thought experiment: Let your imagination run wild about where your career might take you from this point forward, but do it step-by-step. Start with where you are now and think of some possible next steps (school, job, etc). Leave yourself open to unique opportunities that are outside of what you might expect. Now choose one of these imaginary options—it doesn't matter which one—and envision yourself taking it. Now envision the next step. Repeat the process as far into the future as you dare to go.

4. Reflect on your experience of the thought experiment in Question 3. How does the person at the end of your imaginary career relate to the person you are

now? Can you recognize them? Do they inspire you? Do they scare you?

5. Think of a person in your life whom you feel best embodies a growth mindset. What made you think of them?

6. Extra Credit: Set up a time to speak with the person you chose above about their career and their life.

Notes

Introduction

1. https://www.michaelpage.co.in/sites/michaelpage.co.in/files/15507_IN_Employee%20Intentions%20Report_FINAL_0.pdf
2. https://www.unicef.org/globalinsight/media/2266/file
3. https://www.indiatoday.in/education-today/news/story/93-indian-students-aware-of-just-seven-career-options-what-are-parents-doing-wrong-1446205-2019-02-04
4. https://www.wired.com/story/impatient-with-colleges-employers-design-their-own-courses/?xid=PS_smithsonian

Chapter 1: You Can Do Anything

1. https://www.pnas.org/doi/10.1073/pnas.1011492107
2. https://www.wundermanthompson.com/insight/new-trend-report-generation-z-building-a-better-normal

3. https://www.newindianexpress.com/magazine/2021/aug/08/well-established-careers-are-left-behind-to-follow-passion-amid-pandemic-2340723.html

4. https://journals.sagepub.com/doi/abs/10.1177/0956797618780643

5. https://cdn2.hubspot.net/hubfs/481927/Randstad%20Workmonitor%20global%20report%20Q4%20-%20Dec%202019.pdf?__hstc=243245085.1379a85d4c0d338d8bd4bad57ed93ee0.1591170826568.1591170826568.1591170826568.1&__hssc=243245085.2.1591170826568

6. https://www.michaelpage.co.in/sites/michaelpage.co.in/files/15507_IN_Employee%20Intentions%20Report_FINAL_0.pdf

Chapter 2: It All Starts with Self-Discovery

1. https://www.linkedin.com/pulse/20130917155206-69244073-say-goodbye-to-mbti-the-fad-that-won-t-die/

2. https://others.thehighereducationreview.com/news/indian-students-show-high-resilience-to-pressure-with-an-active-schedule-nid-735.html#:~:text=Almost%20two%2Dthirds%20of%20Indian,play%20sports%20regularly%20in%20school.

Chapter 3: Balancing Breadth and Depth

1. https://www.education.gov.in/sites/upload_files/mhrd/files/NEP_Final_English_0.pdf

2. https://indiaeducationforum.org/pdf/ISR-2021.pdf
3. https://www.nature.com/articles/s41562-021-01062-3#rightslink
4. https://www.thehighereducationreview.com/opinion/last-word/-liberal-arts-education-in-india-the-past-present-and-the-future-fid-28.html
5. https://www.iecabroad.com/blog/the-2020-trend-for-indian-students-studying-abroad/
6. https://www.aeccglobal.in/blog/91-percentage-of-indian-students-prefer-to-study-abroad-in-2021-regardless-of-covid-19
7. https://www.nytimes.com/2019/09/20/business/liberal-arts-stem-salaries.html
8. https://www.census.gov/programs-surveys/acs/data/data-tables.html

Chapter 4: Focusing on the Right Skills

1. https://wheebox.com/static/wheebox_pdf/india-skills-report-2018.pdf
2. https://www.odu.edu/content/dam/odu/offices/cmc/docs/nace/2019-nace-job-outlook-survey.pdf
3. https://www.forbes.com/sites/nazbeheshti/2018/09/24/are-hard-skills-or-soft-skills-more-important-to-be-an-effective-leader/?sh=4bada5aa2eb3
4. https://www.nber.org/papers/w21473
5. https://professional.dce.harvard.edu/blog/emotional-intelligence-is-no-soft-skill/#:~:text=In%20fact%2C%20emotional%20intelligence%E2%80%

94the%20ability%20to%2C%20for%20instance,
Business%20Review%2C%20January%202004).

6. https://reports.weforum.org/outlook-global-agenda-2015/

Chapter 5: Picking Up (and Connecting) the Dots

1. https://www.nvp.com/ceojourneystudy/#fear-of-failure

2. Sitkin, S. (1996). Learning through failure: The strategy of small losses. In M. D. Cohen & L. S. Sproull (Eds.), *Organizational Learning* (pp. 541–577). Thousand Oaks, CA: SAGE Publications, Inc.

3. Sakulku, J. (2011). The Impostor Phenomenon. *The Journal of Behavioral Science*, 6(1), 75–97. https://doi.org/10.14456/ijbs.2011.6

4. https://www.ncbi.nlm.nih.gov/pmc/articles/PMC7703426/

5. https://www.youtube.com/watch?v=ZfKMq-rYtnc

6. https://papers.ssrn.com/sol3/papers.cfm?abstract_id=1308286

7. https://hbr.org/2018/09/the-business-case-for-curiosity

Chapter 6: The Power of Mentorship

1. https://knowledge.wharton.upenn.edu/article/workplace-loyalties-change-but-the-value-of-mentoring-doesnt/

2. https://www.vistage.com/research-center/personal-development/leadership-mentoring/

3. https://www.cnbc.com/2019/07/16/nine-in-10-workers-who-have-a-mentor-say-they-are-happy-in-their-jobs.html
4. https://www.ncbi.nlm.nih.gov/pmc/articles/PMC 7642471/
5. https://www.mentorcliq.com/blog/mentoring-stats
6. https://www.thehindu.com/education/how-can-law-students-can-maximise-the-benefits-of-mentorship/article37931506.ece
7. https://radar.brookes.ac.uk/radar/items/4cc1cad3-d410-4358-980e-13370b15a9a8/1/
8. https://www.shrm.org/resourcesandtools/hr-topics/organizational-and-employee-development/pages/generation-z-seeks-guidance-in-the-workplace.aspx
9. https://www.forbes.com/sites/barnabylashbrooke/2019/06/21/want-more-from-generation-z-mentor-dont-manage-them/?sh=458bd4575530

Chapter 7: Advice for Parents: Tapping into the Secret Sauce

1. https://www.macrotrends.net/countries/IND/india/gdp-gross-domestic-product
2. https://www.amazon.com/World-Flat-History-Twenty-first-Century/dp/0374292884
3. https://ncrb.gov.in/en/accidental-deaths-suicides-india-2019
4. https://www.thehindu.com/news/national/student-suicides-rising-28-lives-lost-every-day/article30685085.ece

5. https://www2.deloitte.com/content/dam/Deloitte/
    in/Documents/about-deloitte/in-deloitte-millennial-
    survey-2021-India-report-noexp.pdf
6. https://www.washingtonpost.com/news/morning-
    mix/wp/2015/01/16/bollywood-superstar-deepika-
    padukone-reveals-her-struggle-with-depression/
7. https://news.ucsc.edu/2017/06/singh-book.html
8. https://www.dukece.com/insights/how-indian-
    education-produces-sky-high-achievers/

Conclusion: Unlocking a Growth Mindset

1. https://www.cnbc.com/2022/06/01/netflix-co-
    founder-marc-randolph-follow-your-dreams-is-bad-
    advice.html
2. Carol S. Dweck, PhD, 2007, *Mindset: The New
    Psychology of Success*, Ballantine Books
3. https://hbr.org/2016/01/what-having-a-growth-
    mindset-actually-means